$ELL THE PIG

Stories
of an
Accidental
Gold
Miner

ALAN FARMER

ISBN-13: 978-1511976794
ISBN-10: 1511976799

Lewis Carroll was the pseudonym of Charles Dodgson who taught mathematics at Christ Church College, Oxford University for most of his adult life. One summer day in 1862 Dodgson took eleven year old Alice Liddell and her two sisters for a boat ride. To wile away the time he told them a tale about a girl named Alice who had adventures that grew 'curiouser and curiouser.' Three and a half years later *Alice's Adventures in Wonderland* was published.

ACKNOWLEDGMENTS

For Helen Oxenbury (Author) and her wonderful
children's book *Alice's Adventures in Wonderland*.

For Al Frame (the sharp eyed broker) A friend in need is a
friend indeed.

For Jim (the trader) who flew too close to the Sun.

For Don Valentine (the grouse shooter) who
hung in there, when all appeared lost.

For Kent McGrew (the mad scientist) who worried the gold
from rock.

For John Taylor (the clever geologist) who
made a truly fabulous gold mine.

For all those wonderful miners (my friends) who
had faith in an accidental gold miner.

For John May (deal maker supreme) and his recollections
of Hemlo and the last Gold Rush of the 20th Century.

For Ed Parker (the spin man) and his tales of The Bay Street Boys

For Kim Kulla-Farmer (Graphic Artist) and her
endless patience with a digital dummy.

For Ed Jenne (Illustrator) for his wonderful cover illustration.

For Derek Heckman (Editor) for editing my manuscript.

For my Readers and Editors for having faith in a neophyte.

PREFACE:

I BECAME A GOLD MINER BY ACCIDENT.

At the time, I was an entrepreneur trading oil properties. It was a high-risk business requiring nerves of steel, but it was also very rewarding, assuming the Gods came down on your side when the accounting was complete. Marc Rich—another oil trader, and founder of trading giant Glencore—once told a friend "a trader walks on the blade, so best not to fall off." Definitely good advice for anyone thinking of taking up trading commodities as a profession.

I became an entrepreneur because I had trouble with the rigid authority of the corporate world and made the mistake of treading on the wrong toes. I came from a very ordinary background and had a second-class education that trained me for nothing. But I was young and full of enthusiasm and, as luck would have it, met the right people at the right time, and they opened my eyes to the exciting possibilities open to those willing to 'walk on the edge of the blade'.

One of these fellow-walkers, and the man who would become my partner, was a trader whose best advice was never to buy anything unless you knew who to sell it to (hopefully before you owned it). He would underline this belief by advising all who would listen to 'sell the pig!' Unfortunately, in the case of our Great Gold Caper, we failed to heed this advice and, as a consequence, spent three years involved in a business where there were seemingly no rules.

I had never seen anything like the gold business. It was both surreal and chaotic, almost like the Mad Hatter's Tea Party in Lewis Carroll's wonderful tales of Alice in Wonderland.

At the outset, I understood little of what was happening, maybe by design of my partners, who had their own agenda. By the end, I knew too much, and I paid the price. But I learned a lot about the business (some good, some bad) as I did about the darker side of human nature. I also got to know some of the most fascinating characters imaginable, as well the gold miners who made it all possible.

It was an exciting time to be in the business because of the Hemlo Discovery, which set in motion the last gold rush of the 20th century, and because all this happened in a time before the stifling regulation that has now run the mining business into the ground. It was also a period of 'irrational exuberance' for my partners in the securities business, who it seemed, could raise capital for the goofiest schemes at the drop of a hat.

These times have unfortunately passed by, so we are left with the memories of those such as myself who were there and lived to tell about it.

Some of these stories are not new and may have been written about by others. Regardless they represent my take on the events as they occurred, or, as in some cases, as I heard them from those directly involved.

Gold and ethics remain, as ever, strange bedfellows, and the future for the business is as murky as ever. But somehow, when the next great gold discovery is made, I doubt the results will be very different.

Finally, I have bought this story of Gold up-to-date by means of a chapter entitled "The Skin of the Gods" which should provide a small glimpse into the future.

* * *

1

"The times has come," the Walrus said,
"To talk of many things:
Of shoes—and ships—and ceiling wax—
Of cabbages—and kings— "

From *Through the Looking Glass*, Lewis Carroll

OCTOBER 29, 1987:

THE BLACK HILLS OF SOUTH DAKOTA are famous but certainly not beautiful. They derive their name from the Sioux Indians who saw the dark shadow cast by the rounded hills as they rode the great Upland Plains, later to become the State of Wyoming.

The hills bear the scars of the many small gold mines that sprung up after the discovery of a giant gold ingot in a mountain stream and the subsequent Dakota Territory Gold Rush of the 1870's.

No event in American history gave rise to more infamous characters or more history. The town of Deadwood, now a gambling Mecca, still claims the likes of Wild Bill Hickok and Calamity Jane as its own. General Custer, who is said to have been present when the ingot was found, will forever be linked to the area through his work opening the great Northwest Plains to settlers and prospectors.

The Dakota Gold Rush was unique in another fashion. Unlike California in 1849 and some other gold discoveries in the American West, it gave rise to a long-term mining industry that would eventually employ thousands of miners and create billions of dollars in real wealth.

The head-frame of the greatest gold mine in the history of the United States, and maybe the World, still stands in the apply-named town of Lead (pronounced "leed") South Dakota. Owned by the Homestake Mining Company, one of the first mining companies to have its shares listed on the New York Stock Exchange, this deep mine produced over four million ounces of gold during its 120-year lifespan.

Still based in San Francisco as a result of its long-time ownership by the family of William Randolph Hurst, in 1986 this mining company was considered by many to be the Rolls Royce of the gold miners.

I was visiting the Black Hills on Monday October 29, 1987,because through a combination of incredible luck, good judgment, and plain pecuniary necessity, I had acquired a great deal of gold from this famous old company for a price that would later attract a lot of attention.

The story of how I was able to do this really begins two-and-a-half billion years ago when a huge volcano spewed molten lava from deep within the earth across a desolate landscape that showed no signs of life.

The magma contained masses of iron, which, in its elemental form, carried gold and other precious metals that would, over the process of time, be deposited in fissures and veins in the cooling host rocks. In the case of the Homestake Mine, these fissures would later be traced by ingenious miners over eight thousand feet below the surface through a labyrinth of shafts and tunnels.

The giant volcano would burp its gaseous brew many more times, each time melting the surrounding rock and re-mobilizing the gold trapped in the rock fissures.

It was this re-mobilized gold that would become the cause of a second Dakota Gold Rush in the 1980's and allow me to make what would turn out to be one of the better deals in the lore of gold.

Geology can be a subjective subject, and the history of mineral discoveries is full of rebels willing to flaunt the current geological dogma. My case would prove no different.

I was president of a failed gold-mining company a hair removed from insolvency. Like so many others, we had tried and failed to coax enough gold from oxidized rock in the Black Hills of South Dakota so as to become more than a nuisance.

Out of both money and the patience of our long-suffering investors, we had drilled into an adjacent property as a last ditch effort and, as the saying goes, had 'come up lucky'. The problem was that we did not own the minerals under the land we had drilled and had only a tenuous claim to the surface, which was riddled with old mining shafts and muddled ownership. This is not a healthy situation at the best of times, but when gold is involved it can be down right ugly.

The mineral claims we had drilled into dated back prior to South Dakota's statehood and were currently owned by a wealthy playboy who, when not shooting Grouse in Scotland or fly fishing in Iceland, liked to enjoy the good life. It was said that he had purchased the property from the bankrupt estate of a defunct mining company as a refuge for wild turkeys.

He took as a partner an irascible old gold miner who proved very difficult to get along with. The old man, who would later marry his secretary at the age of eighty, had been around the area for a very long time, but he had failed to stop hippie squatters from settling on the land. As a result, the chain of title for the huge surrounding area was at best, a muddle, and at worst, a complete disaster.

Old mineral claims involving gold are complicated beasts that frequently involve disputes and over-staking, which can lead to fractional claims and all kinds of other liens. Among those with recorded ownership to the claims we had drilled into was the Homestake Mining Company, which owned the company store when it came to gold mining claims in the Black Hills of South Dakota. Since our road to salvation went through that company store, the task of getting the rascals to the bargaining table fell to me.

As luck would have it, a solution presented itself in the form a very bright young geological engineer who had latched onto the concept of re-mobilized gold in the Black Hills and was prepared to stake his reputation on the outcome. Since he was the kind of young man who would drive a hundred miles to get a bottle of wine for dinner and could also explain the complex details of geological exploration to a trader such as myself, I figured rightly that he was an ideal candidate to lead the charge.

After ranting to the Homestake senior management in San Francisco for a few months, I had finally succeeded in getting their desk-bound geologists to pay us a visit and allow our young gold guru to do his thing. It was an impressive presentation with enough technical data to satisfy the experts and wow almost any investor, but apparently not geologists steeped in the history of gold in Lawrence County, South Dakota. I had been forewarned by some wise old men of such possible intransigence and had been advised to let the charade play out. It would have been plain daft to build up the value of possible gold still in the ground if there was a serious intention to try and buy the claims. There was also the nagging question as to whether, having purchased whatever gold might be present, we would ever be given the chance to mine the claims. Long gone were the days when ownership of minerals came with the right to extract them—a difficult fact to accept since much of the Black Hills looked like the surface of the moon. Now mining permits could easily become the subject of fierce battles fought in the glare of public opinion, and where the outcome was often politically motivated. Finally, there was the seemingly difficult question of money, or the apparent lack thereof. Here, the advantage in the David-and-Goliath struggle swung to our side, for few people, other than myself, knew what could be done if we could consolidate the competing interests in all the claims and obtain a mining permit.

In the business of gold, unlike poker, a player is not required to show his stake or his cards. In this case, I had already bought into the reality that the gold was present and that it could be worth a great deal of money. More importantly, some real experts agreed and were prepared to give the blessing required to bring in new investors with lots of money. Thus, if the hubris of the Homestake team was great enough it was best to let them get on with it.

When I was invited back to San Francisco, it became readily apparent that the grand ruse had worked in our favor. The desk-bound geologists obviously did not believe we had the gold, or that it was worth much, for their offer contained a figure I never would have thought possible for all of their company's mineral interests in a huge block of claims in the Black Hills. So I took the offer and ran.

There is nothing in the world like gold. If you have gold or, if greedy buggers think you have gold, they will beat a path to your door. In our case, the greedy buggers believed we had a million ounces of the stuff, and that was enough to get the ball rolling. As it would turn out, our gold guru was proved right, and there was a lot more gold than even the most optimistic promoter could have imagined—a likelihood that would hasten our downfall rather than guarantee success.

The first nine months of 1987 were a blur. The drill bit had apparently converted our ugly duckling into a swan, and now everyone wanted a piece of the action. More rare than gold itself is the small company that defies the odds and makes a gold mine by itself. After three years of rejection by partners and investors alike, we had apparently achieved this unlikely result. But, unfortunately, we had forgotten the possibility that villains were watching and, honoring a long tradition with gold, were ready to pounce if the opportunity were to present itself.

I was in the Black Hills that day to witness the magical production of a few bars of gold from thousands of tons of rock that is the business of the modern day gold mine. Our mine for the first time had begun to produce gold bars at a cost that would ensure a big profit for me and our new partners, thus fulfilling a promise made to my new shareholders. The success was particularly sweet for me since I had managed to outsmart my former partners who had, unceremoniously, dumped me and sold out to another gold mining company at a give-away price without so much as a day's notice. Not a good way to part company after three years of hard work and a miraculous redemption.

Then came the fateful phone message advising of the Stock Market meltdown that would come to be called Black Monday. By the end of the day, our company would be worth only one third of what it had been the previous Friday, an event which would trigger a bitter take-over squabble that would bring an abrupt and unhappy end to my gold mining days. A further consequence of this debacle was that I had managed to lose fourteen million dollars from my own account

My partners had long lost interest in our investment and had decided to "sell the pig" at the very time they should have been buying. Not willing to give away a "sure thing," I had arranged to place my partners' shares with other investors and, as a gesture of good faith, had "gone long" and bought some shares for my own account. The only problem was, if the shares went down in value, as opposed to up, I would have no means to pay for them. Until that day, the shares had only gone up in value, so I had not been concerned and looked forward to a big score in return for all of my efforts. Now, panic-selling on a market with only a single buyer had apparently cast this possibility in grave doubt.

The buyer of all our shares was another gold company with a complicated ownership, managed by an accountant with a big ego and a fat wallet. The company was an historic gold miner that had made millions of dollars from a famous mine in Red Lake, Ontario. Much of the cash derived from this long time endeavor was still in the treasury and available to finance the purchase of our undervalued shares. More sinister was the connection between our two gold companies and the Merchant Bank, which had financed me and our new gold mine. Word had it that they also had an historic relationship with our suitor.

Who would the Merchant Bank support? Me, or the accountant and the famous gold miner with all the cash? Experienced gained from my relationship with partners who were feared for their cut-throat dealings in the Stock Market told me that, despite assurances to the contrary, enlightened self-interest would rule the day. My interest at least was clear: I must to buy time and find a friendly buyer, a White Knight who would trump the bid of our opportunistic suitor and bail me out from my precarious financial position.

* * *

2

Will you, won't you, will you, won't you, will you join the dance?

−From Alice's Adventures in Wonderland, Lewis Carroll

THE DANCE:

IT STARTED WITH ONE OF THOSE PHONE CALLS, the unexpected ones that leave you cold and baffled. When I answered the phone, a chick with a clipped British accent told me to please hold for "Mr. C," also known to me as Sell-the-Pig Jimmy." Jim was a hard-driving, martini-drinking friend who ran a very successful financial house in Toronto. I knew very little of his business, other than what I had read in the financial press. Apparently, he was a rising star in the merchant-banking world who had some very rich and powerful backers.

I have always had trouble accepting that anyone was too busy to make their own phone calls, and Jim sure as hell did not have to put on airs with me. Perhaps he meant in this case to convey the message that I had better give him what he wanted.

Jimmy came on the line and immediately started barking that he needed my services as a partner in a trade involving the shares of a small gold company he had purchased from a large bank to whom he owed a favor. Nothing new there. Then the message became garbled. Apparently the shares in question represented effective control of the gold company and formed part of the bank's security for loans made to a third party that had been "called" In other words, another company had used the shares as a form of payment against loans owed to the bank, likely in order to avoid bankruptcy.

Jim went on to tell me we would avoid messy dealings with regulators by having four silent partners, of which I would be one. I vaguely knew the others as names that had been involved in some big deals, which had stood the financial community on its ear. In a bizarre twist, the president of the debtor company was included with the deal and, as a consolation prize, was to become president of our gold company. Finally, assuming I would help him out, he would instruct his bank office to send me confirmation of the trade and an invoice for an amount of money I had never and likely would never be offered again—did not have and likely never would.

I have often wondered what would have happened if I had taken the prudent course and demurred pending further information. But this is not how things were done in Jim's world, and I suppose being included with some big names impressed me. So he got what he thought he wanted, and I got what would turn out to be a long-term pain in the ass.

In near panic, I began a frantic search for information on our new prize. I called the soon-to-be president, who we will call Peter, and after his long rant on the unfairness of life and banks who wanted their money back, I received the promise of every scrap of information on the gold company. I found it strange that he would convey his visceral dislike for the financial community in general, and in particular for "Sell-the-Pig Jim" to me. Perhaps his attempt to shoot the messenger should have been fair warning that the plan hatched by the bank would not sit well with the partners, or with the employees of the gold company. But right then I had bigger problems in just how to come up with the money I now owed Jim.

The stagflation experienced during the 1970's had led to an unprecedented increase in gold prices, an unusual happenstance that had sent geologists with any knowledge of gold properties scurrying around trying to stake, or otherwise acquire, properties with even a hint of gold. The new in-vogue idea was "heap leaching," a process that was able to treat oxidized gold ores without expensive milling. The major mining companies had looked at the idea and mostly passed, leaving the field open to hundreds of smaller companies to try their hand. Apparently, our small gold mine was one such company.

A retired but long-respected American geologist had acquired several heap leach gold properties in South Dakota and Montana and had resold them to small public companies in return for shares and a gross royalty on any gold produced. We were one of his prospective companies.

The idea to match technical know-how with the ability to raise capital was a good one, provided the dichotomy between the two disciplines could be reconciled. Promoters who were known to use highly unorthodox methods of raising capital often ran small public companies. A good promoter would all too often promise the moon and fall short on delivery, leaving the technicians high and dry. Likewise, the technicians would overestimate the gold present and underestimate the amount of money needed to produce the metal.

The published information sent to me was high on promotion and low on detail, leading me to suspect our small gold company might not be quite what was promised.

In the past, I had borrowed a lot of money from big banks and, by stint of luck and timing—the most important ingredients of any deal—had repaid every penny. Banks were keen on people like me because we generated big fees and fat bonuses, provided they could be assured the risk lay with others. It was nearly always better to own all of what was being traded and offset the risk by a short sale than to own a small part and take the risk of not selling at all. A banker who had smuggled gold out of Havana in order save it from the grasp of Fidel Castro once told me that a good banker should put his eggs in one basket and watch the basket like hell.

In the case of my new partners, I was beginning to suspect neither the eggs nor the basket were to my liking. It had now been a week since the call from Jim and, as promised, I had received the details of my purported share purchase. But I still hadn't gotten any new information about the trade, or on how we would sell the pig. So I decided to see for myself what was going on with our gold mine.

I chartered a plane for a trip to the Black Hills and browbeat our reluctant president, Peter, into accompanying me. Our flight took us to Rapid City where we rented a car for the trip to Deadwood and a meeting with an heir of the deceased owner who we will call Dale. Along the way, the discussion got around to the bad blood that obviously existed between the financiers and the operators of the mine due to broken promises from both sides. Simply put, there was not enough money or gold to go around.

When we finally located the mine, it became obvious that we all had a big problem: the operation was in imminent danger of shutting down from lack of funds, and consequently, no one was happy. Gold miners were used to this kind of situation and could be tolerant up to a point, but when the paycheck bounced, it usually signaled the end, and they would go to work for the next group of optimists.

Another problem was that there were too many chiefs and not enough Indians. Our host Dale was a non-resident manager who commuted by way of his own private plane. He also had a staff of professionals at his beck and call who were paid for by our insolvent gold miner. Small wonder there was no money left in the till. Despite all these obstacles, I was assured that more money would produce more gold and all would be well. Just where this money was to come from was now apparently my problem. I also learned that our company was the proud owner of a minority interest in another heap leech gold mine in the Little Rocky Mountains of Montana, one that wasn't producing enough gold to do us any good either. Somehow keeping a straight face, Dale told me we were being royally screwed by the bunch of thieves who were cooking the books, and that we would never receive a dime for all the money that had been invested.

In mining terms, I was now in between a rock and a hard place. I was caught up in a silent partnership that had purchased almost worthless shares in an insolvent company from a very large and powerful bank. I now also knew that our gold company owed the same bank a lot of money, so there was no way the bank could claim ignorance of the precarious nature of their investment. This took me back to Jim. Was it possible that he did not know or care, or was this really payback for another deal? Nothing made much sense except the probability that I was stuck in the middle and owed a lot of money for shares that would be damn difficult to sell.

When I finally managed to snare Jim away from his trading floor for three minutes, I gave him what I thought was the bad news. I did not have the money to pay for the shares and no one in their right mind would lend it to me. Without missing a beat, he told me not to worry. He would be my banker and give me the same terms as he got from his backers. Furthermore, he was not interested in the messy details. Those were being taken care of by another one of his partners. End of story.

Now I knew for sure I was in way over my head and might be in danger of becoming a pawn in whatever the grand scheme was. I had heard all about the partner in charge of details, who was also known as "The Shark." He was a mercurial type who operated in the shadows and almost never showed his public face. He was also one of those strange people who would carry on a conversation in words of one syllable, leaving his listeners to try and figure what he meant. If "The Shark" was calling the shots then someone was going to be required to front for him.

Suddenly I realized that someone could well be me.

* * *

3

The Queen of Hearts
She made some tarts,
All on a summer's day;
The Knave of Hearts
He stole those tarts,
And took them clean away.

– From *Alice's Adventures in Wonderland,* Lewis Carroll

EMPTY HANDED:

I WAS NOW A DIRECTOR OF AN INSOLVENT GOLD COMPANY that owed its soul and all of its gold to the bank. This was the same bank that had sold me, and my partners, the almost worthless shares that we now owned. I seldom heard from my partners and had to rely on sporadic missives from their appointee to the board of directors, a pedantic asshole, whom I presumed was there to keep an eye on me in case I stepped out of line.

Our gold mine was not producing enough gold to pay the bank and we had only the word of Dale, who had also been contracted to manage the operation—that the situation could be saved by throwing more money into the mix. Peter, our bank-appointed President, was an ex-oilman who knew nothing about gold or gold mining, and who spent his working days kibitzing with his stock-broker cronies about how he had been screwed out of his just rewards by a bank that had the temerity to ask for it's loans to be repaid on time and with interest.

There was little doubt that we were another example of a public gold company being managed as the personal fiefdom of the previous owners. They had sold the mining rights for a whole lot of shares in the company and would now receive a handsome royalty from any gold produced. It fell to me to break the news to the two protagonists that play time in the sandlot was over and the cost of their folly would be a new owner, one who would demand much higher costs of capital than were customary for potential gold mining companies.

'The Shark' had temporally emerged from the shadows with an offer to lend the company the money required to repay the bank loans. It would also provide the capital required to increase gold production to a level that would render the operation capable of generating interest on his new loans, while leaving existing shareholders with nothing. In order to tidy up a potentially messy situation, existing shareholders were to be given the chance to participate in the new financing, albeit only after having the chance to study documents that would spell out for the first time the precarious nature of the company's financial situation. This offer represented the only game in town and looked like a potential rescue for a board of directors charged with the fiduciary responsibility of keeping the company solvent in the face of blatant misinformation in the public domain.

To "The Shark" it must have appeared otherwise for his sidekick had now seen fit to let me in on the master plan. This was to combine our small refinanced gold mine with other small gold-miners in order to form a bigger ball of wax that could then be sold at a handsome profit. So this, finally, was the planned trade in which I was about to become a not-so-silent partner.

At a hastily convened board meeting, Peter decided to commit management suicide by informing his two new directors that "The Shark's" offer was a blatant attempt to steal the company from unsuspecting shareholders, and that we were somehow part of a plot to manipulate the price of the company's shares to "The Shark's" advantage. To no one's surprise, within a week Peter was relieved of his duties and, amid a flurry of threatened litigation, I was parachuted in as a very unwilling and unpaid replacement.

When a small public company, especially a gold company, plans to raise money from its shareholders or others, it attracts the attention of a whole host or regulators. Suddenly all the sins of the past must be rectified. Despite protestations that all information is provided solely for the benefit of investors, this is seldom the case. What is really involved is a "cover-your-ass" exercise for the regulators and the accountants. With a gold mine, the process is especially complicated since very few understand the arcane descriptions provided by engineers and accountants.

It was very unlikely that "The Shark" understood, and if he did, it was because his own mining analysts had fed him a bunch of platitudes. In a crash course on the realities of the mining business provided to me by experienced miners whom I had known and worked with, I learned all too well the risks involved. A deposit that contains gold is worth nothing if it cannot be mined at a profit. In the case of our small company we had reports completed by serious-minded consultants that said we had two viable gold deposits. One was in the Black Hills and was supposed to be producing quite a lot of gold.

Instead it was producing very little gold and struggling to stay afloat. The other deposit was in the Little Rocky Mountains where the books said we owned an inventory of gold that, according to our partners— we might never get our hands on.

"The Shark's" plan to combine small gold mines into one big-mine depended on the dubious proposition that it is always possible to find a bigger fool if you look hard enough. The alternative was to find gold companies run by like-minded management who would assume greater risks in return for an unknown result in the future. My experience told me that knowledgeable managers would be very unlikely to buy into a company with the limited prospects of our little mine.

As it would turn out, my experience had almost no place in the master plan already decided upon by "The Shark" and his cohorts. My job it seemed was to keep the troops happy until a suitable dance partner was found. I quickly realized that a real dichotomy existed between the promoters and the miners. Luckily for me we had some talented people who, given the chance, could make our gold mine in the Black Hills work. It was more a question of convincing the scientists and engineers we were serious, that we wanted to make a success out of the operation and not just promote our shares.

Extracting minute quantities of gold from millions of tons of rock was a job for experts and not an easy task. It could also be dangerous and hazardous to the environment. Environmental concerns in South Dakota were well-founded: take the debacle of mining giant Homestake poisoning cows twenty miles from its deep mine by discharging mercury into groundwater as an example of why.

The recent case of the Summitville Mine high in the Rocky Mountains was enough to scare the hell out of the officers and directors of small mining companies. In this remote region, minute quantities of cyanide were detected leaking from the abandoned workings. The Environmental Protection Agency laid criminal charges against the bankrupt mining company's former president who had promptly debunked to Singapore. The draconian penalties applicable to the directors of any company that screwed up were no laughing matter, and made any kind of "director's insurance" an impossible dream. I suspected my partners had been well-advised to stay away from direct involvement in the workings of our company.

The arrival of summer and a lot more money began to make a difference and losses were stemmed to a trickle. But gold prices were not cooperating, and so generating enough cash to pay the interest on loans was still an issue. "The Shark'" was now in full attack mode and desperate to find other gold-miners who would buy or merge with our little company. The plethora of mine visits and announcements showed signs of desperation, leaving me to wonder if the Emperor had no clothes and we would have to find another way out of our dilemma.

* * *

"Take some more tea," the March Hare said to Alice, very earnestly.

"I've had nothing yet," Alice replied in an offended tone, "so I can't take more."

"You mean you can't take *less*," said the Hatter:

"it's very easy to take *more* than nothing."

"Nobody asked *your* opinion," said Alice."

–From *Alice's Adventures in Wonderland,* Lewis Carroll

THE PROBLEM OF PEGASUS:

I AM AT A LOSS TO EXPLAIN TIMES IN MY LIFE when, out of the blue, a winning idea has come to me. Maybe it's because I am a believer in the old adage that, when in doubt, you throw a whole bunch of shit at the wall in the hope that something will stick. This is certainly what happened to me in the Great Gold Caper.

I was thrashing around trying to stay out of the way of "The Shark" as he pursued his plans for the grand ensemble of small gold companies, something that, in my mind, was not going to happen. This wasn't because the idea was bad; it was not, but because of the innate fear potential bedmates had for "The Shark" and "Sell-the-Pig Jim," both well-known for their cutthroat behavior, even in a business where nice guys finished last. Small gold mines only existed at all because they were run by fiercely independent managers and owners—capable of staying one step ahead of the promoters and thieves that inhabited the territory. Big mining companies made a business of gobbling up smaller companies who had successfully suffered through the appalling odds of finding and financing a mine. So the appearance of a financier with a slick scheme to make everyone rich was not seen as manna from heaven, but as a threat to their continued existence. Another stumbling block was that "The Shark" knew nothing about mining and relied on an analyst who also knew very little but pretended he did. This made for very difficult communication to the extent that most of the time I had no idea what was going on. I remember once receiving a phone call from a stock broker asking me what I thought of the idea of merging our company with another mine, leaving me in no doubt that the seed had been planted by one of "The Shark's" assistants who was looking for my response. A strange way to run what was fast becoming an auction.

In a moment of short-lived sanity, "The Shark', accompanied by his entourage, decided to make a flying visit to our mining properties in South Dakota and Montana. The Montana visit was my first to this huge mine and would confirm in my own mind that we were being royally screwed by our partners whose only real interest was in the promotion of their company, Pegasus. The visit was a made into a bizarre experience, first by the sheer terror of flying in a small plane in a howling wind into a grass strip in the mountains at Landusky, Montana, and second by the secrecy that prevailed during the visit. In essence, we never got to see anything of substance and certainly no gold. What we did see was a contractor's hundred ton trucks hurtling along on dusty roads to deposit their loads on huge piles of large rocks that were supposed to contain minute gold particles. The gold was to be recovered by spraying the rock piles with a weak solution of sodium cyanide over a period of five years, a delay that would cause grievous environmental problems and lead to a filing for bankruptcy.

"The Shark" apparently thought it was all great and seemed pleased with his visit and with the glowing promise of lots of gold. I think he had Pegasus in mind for a buyer or bedmate, a truly scary thought. My take was very different—for I now knew we were an unwilling participant in an advanced accounting fraud. Simply put, the idea of the Pegasus promoters was to invent a large inventory of phantom gold that could then be used to raise the capital to buy a real source of gold. This novel approach was made possible by bogus metallurgy: reported laboratory tests indicated that even the lowest values of contained gold could be recovered over long periods without the need for crushing and milling the rock. This apparently was enough for the auditors to report a very large inventory of gold and thus to defer a large part of the mining costs. It was pretty obvious to my crew, including a very clever metallurgical engineer, that the gold would never be recovered in our lifetime.

The discovery of this obviously fraudulent scheme presented some real problems for me. We had refinanced our company based upon audited financial statements that showed a value for the phantom gold of Pegasus. What would happen if this large value just disappeared, as obviously it would have to? Making matters worse was that we had been told about the potential problem by one of our founding shareholders and had done nothing.

The answer to this dilemma was not pretty, but I knew instinctively what had to be done. We had to sell our interest to Pegasus using the threat of exposure as a club in order to get a price that would not embarrass "The Shark" and his partners. The only way this could be done was to sell our interest in the scheme for real gold bullion.

I had met some rogues in the mining business, but no one who could compare to the major domo of Pegasus. He was a bad actor who, amongst other things, had been banned for life by the SEC from being a director or officer of any public company. He sat in an office just down the hall from the legitimate officers of the company and obviously ran the show from the shadows, all rather like a Godfather. I had elected to meet him alone for the obvious reason that things might be said that would need to be deniable if necessary.

In the ensuing game of bullshit poker, I had a good hand because I could use the fearsome reputation of my partners as a club even though they likely did not understand why I had decided to go head-to-head with Pegasus, a well-known gold-miner. It was also a good sign that the Godfather had emerged from the shadows long enough to keep his grand ruse on the tracks. It did not matter who was right or wrong, just so long as a deal was struck. The most difficult part was figuring out how to structure the purchase so Pegasus could direct the spin away from the real reason for the deal.

It may well have been an example of a deal with the devil, but it was set up so that, in return for keeping our mouths shut, we would get an agreed volume of real bullion delivered over a five year period. When all of the gold had been delivered, the surface and mineral rights of the mine would revert to Pegasus. A subsequent finesse was required to bring "The Shark" on board, after he mused that he perhaps should get the Pegasus gold bullion. No such explanation was required for our mining crew; the deal showed our willingness to build something real as opposed to promotional horseshit and it started to move forward on all fronts.

It must have been at this point that I also crossed the invisible line from trader to someone willing to work his ass off for an uncertain reward. In so doing, I committed the cardinal sin for a trader—I became emotionally involved. It was also fun because I now had a crew that was prepared to teach me how to find and mine gold successfully. Just as significant, I now had people I could shoot the bull with—as opposed to listening to "The Shark's" endless questionable schemes.

The most important place in a gold property is the laboratory where hundreds of rock samples are tested every day. The laboratory results tell the operators where they are in a deposit that has already been outlined by drilling hundreds of holes and thousands of assays. Drilling is controlled by on-site geologists, or metallurgists, who have as their goal a material balance of exactly how many ounces of gold, are in the recovery system at any one time. This detail is hard to fathom when the volume of rock mined in a day can be hundreds or even thousands of times the number of ounces that are recovered. The detail is necessary because gold is so valuable, even in minute quantities, and people will steal gold whenever the chance presents itself.

Over time, the ongoing testing and subsequent control greatly reduces the risks of gold mining and thus renders raising capital a lot easier. As we moved forward, it became apparent that we might be mining a small part of a much larger system under adjacent land owned by others. This bought a whole new dynamic to the equation, namely that of building something far larger and a great deal more profitable. Such a determination would normally be very positive for shareholders and new investors alike. To traders such as "Sell the Pig Jim," however, it was incidental and served only to heighten the need to constantly turn the dollars involved for a profit.

This dichotomy put me in the bizarre position of running one way while my partners continued on another. The thought of selling the pig now was even more insane than it had been when we started out. Why sell a wing and a prayer when you can have the real thing? Especially when that real thing is a large gold deposit that could be worth hundreds of millions or even billions of dollars.

As for Pegasus, their schemes apparently went according to plan. The bogus gold inventory allowed the company to borrow one hundred million dollars, a sum that was used to acquire and mine real gold deposits in Montana and Nevada. The company eventually went bankrupt and none of the principals were ever charged. The mines in the Little Rocky Mountains are the subject of continuing remediation by the State to remove residual amounts of sodium cyanide.

* * *

5

"Now, here, you see,
it takes all the running you can do,
to keep in the same place.
If you want to get somewhere else,
you must run at least twice as fast as that!"

– From *Alice Through the Looking Glass,* Lewis Carroll

SAMUEL MONTAGU:

I WAS TOLD BY AN OLD GOLD MINER that, if I was serious about the gold business, I had better spend some time in London, a city considered by many to be the epicenter of the business. The formal business of gold started here in 1750 when the Bank of England, smarting from the debacle of the South Sea Bubble, created the Good Delivery List, a list of refiners who could be trusted to deliver 99.99 % pure gold bullion. One hundred years later, five banks created the London Gold Bullion Market that ran the business for one hundred and thirty years until 1980 when the London Bullion Market Association was formed by the Bank of England. These five banks were led by N.M. Rothschild, the bank that financed Britain in the Napoleonic Wars, and also included others owned by Orthodox Jews, one of which was Samuel Montagu and Co.

Hidden away in the Old City, this historic merchant bank made its name—as well as a fortune for its founder, Samuel Montagu—brokering Australian gold after the Victoria gold rush in the 1850's. In those early days, the spread between buyers and sellers was much wider than it is today, mostly because gold produced by itinerate miners was alluvial and needed to be purified prior to being accepted as bullion or specie. The only accepted refineries were either owned by, or close to, the Bank of England in faraway London. Disputes over assays were common, and gradually the London refineries became the most widely-accepted referees, leading to the birth of a business that survives to this day. This opportunistic merchant bank was accustomed to making huge spreads, a practice that would survive through numerous family trusts for 130 years until the bank itself was acquired by international banking giant HSBC.

Being old and very British, it was impossible to walk past a be-top-hatted and into these hallowed halls, all lined with a fortune in paintings, without a proper introduction. I got my passport from another banker, a member of the European Parliament who also happened to sit on my board of directors as an appointee of "The Shark."

I was looking to lever a receivable of gold bullion from Pegasus against the purchase of leases that might well hold a lot of gold. This was a classic trade involving a good degree of risk with a huge potential return. The idea had come to me through talking with the owners of mineral leases that abutted our gold mine in South Dakota and, in particular, with an old miner who had managed the last operation in the area. My young geologist told me that this crusty old bastard knew a thing or two about gold and how it could be found in great quantities within the shadow of our mine. The results from initial drilling were positive, so we were of one mind that we should acquire the leases from our partner, the Homestake Mining Company, and re-negotiate a lower royalty that reflected our new method of mining.

Gold and silver royalties are considered by many to be the most valuable form of investment, virtually bulletproof from the many thieves that operate in the business. This is because they are gross payments, applicable before mining costs made in gold or silver (or the equivalent), and based on prices indexed to the London Fix at the time of the shipment. A royalty claim is a direct charge on the land or leases and comes before all creditors. Small wonder that they are prized and very difficult to change once in place. The old miner was intransigent, but his partner, a real estate tycoon, was not. He knew of the difficulties in actually producing gold from hundreds of small claims that pre-dated South Dakotan statehood. After mining had ceased, hippie squatters had moved in and earned squatters' rights to ownership of the surface. The mineral rights still belonged to the real estate tycoon. It would prove to be a very complicated business that could well have ended our quest for a huge gold mine had we not obtained the help of a very experienced landowner.

The idea was a bold one, especially for a company that had so recently stood on the precipice of insolvency. To have any chance of success, we had to show that we could raise the capital required to make it all work, hence my pilgrimage to London.

"One who sups with the devil is wise to eat with a long spoon" is a truism that applied in spades when dealing with the Montagu. The deputy chairmen told me after a long lugubrious lunch that the bank expected to make a lot of money dealing with me, a sentiment I did not doubt. These guys were pirates who walked very close to the line—a practice that would eventually cause them grief. I was not a good target because I was dealing with another pirate, "The Shark," who was every bit as greedy. The timing was also wrong, and they may well have had other things on their mind since they had recently been the victims of huge heist of silver ingots from a shipment from London to Germany. After a theft of pure gold or silver, suspicion nearly always falls on the owner because the location and method of shipment are kept secret from everyone else for obvious reasons. Many gold producers ship their gold through the mail because insurance is cheap and the timing is known to only a very few. No matter what, gold and silver remains the number one target of thieves, since once in a pure form (99.99% for gold and 99.95%, for silver) they are universally accepted as specie without too many questions. In the case of the Montagu silver, the sheer bulk of the haul and the information from a turncoat eventually led to the recovery of the silver ingots.

A gold loan should have been the cheapest way to raise capital since it involved the loan of gold bullion that would otherwise sit in a bonded warehouse and be subject to insurance and storage charges payable by the owner. The borrower usually paid these charges and a small rate of interest in return for a loan of the gold. The trick was to outrun the intermediaries who, given the chance, would steal you blind. As a gold trader, the Montagu was definitely an intermediary. They also knew the owners of most of the gold in the world. The rest I did not know until later.

Prior to making any loan involving gold, there is a delicate mating dance involving the production of extremely detailed information on how and where the gold is going to come from to repay the borrowed metal. Since the agent bank is likely taking most of the risk, the disclosures usually stop there, but not, apparently, in this case. Gold mining is a tough, unforgiving business, so gold miners are very much a fraternity and tend to exchange information about all manner of subjects.

I should not have been surprised to learn that confidential details of our proposed gold loan had found their way into the hands of one or more of our much larger competitors. Much of this information was definitely not in the public domain since it was only understood by engineers and scientists and therefore could only have come from the employees of the Montagu who had received it from myself. I had not thought it necessary to make the bank sign a confidentiality agreement since most banks are usually considered to have a fiduciary relationship with their clients, even would-be clients. I was even more surprised to learn that other gold-miners had run the same gauntlet. Apparently the bank was selling the information to would-be acquirers on a conditional basis, usually called success fees. In a subsequent case, the bank would deny culpability, blaming such behavior on a rogue employee, but would still settle out of court to hide the messy details.

I had neither the time nor the resources to fight with London banks, so chalked the whole business up to a valuable lesson in financing potential gold mines. I now had a healthy distrust of financial intermediaries as well as my partners. If I was to pull the rabbit from the hat it was going to have to be done with people I trusted and knew.

The rabbit in the hat, it turned out, would be a friend of a friend going back to my early corporate struggles. Since my indoctrination into the gold business, the financial world had moved on, and the bank that had sold us the mess that was supposed to be a gold mine was now the owner of one of the larger underwriters of mining securities.

The old friend was a senior partner. He knew 'Sell-the-Pig Jim" and "The Shark" and the likelihood of a sale to a new majority owner. He obviously trusted me that we had something real, and that I would not embarrass him in front of his new owner.

It would be the form of the financing that would set us apart from all the others. Once we had done engineering and geological due diligence, we designed a hybrid security that would allow the owners to participate directly with movements in the price of gold while still owning a part of our company. It was a winning combination for us and the buyers and was the forerunner of the Exchange-traded gold shares that would become so popular. It would also set up the right conditions for an arbitrage between the two classes of shares that would save my ass in the difficult situation that was to follow the collapse of financial markets in October of 1987.

* * *

The Queen had only one way of settling all difficulties, great or small. 'Off with his head!' she said, without even looking round.

–From *Alice's Adventures in Wonderland,* Lewis Carroll

THE SALE OF THE PIG:

THERE WAS A TIME IN THE NOT TOO RECENT PAST when I would have been grateful for any satisfactory ending to my insane adventure in the gold business. Now, having overcome incredible odds, and having built a business with real value, I was aghast to learn in an early morning call that "The Shark" had sold all the holdings of the partnership to a group with close financial ties. The price was close to market value but gave no credence to the potential value of the company.

This sudden development was quite legal since the financing partners had the right to pull the sale-trigger at any time and the other partners had the right to match any offer within a forty-eight hour period. There was also a silver lining in the fact that the sale price would cover the debts I had incurred to buy the pig three years before. The really bad news was that the new owners wanted no part of me, so I was to be unceremoniously dumped into the dustbin of history along with all but one of our directors. So when the smoke cleared, I would have worked my ass off and taken incredible risks for no wages only to emerge three years later with nothing. This was a shitty way to treat me and my partners knew it.

"Sell-the-Pig Jim" had gotten us into this mess, likely as a payback favor to a very powerful bank. The outcome could have been much different had "The Shark" completed even one of his asinine schemes but he had not, and it had been left to me alone to sort it all out. It made absolutely no sense to sell when we were on the verge of a very profitable outcome. The risks were seemingly behind us and the value of the company was about to double and at the very least. We had a gold miner's dream because we could produce an ounce of gold for seventy-five dollars, meaning we had one of the lowest cost operations anywhere. Once these economics were realized, the value of the company's shares would rise to reflect the value of proven net gold, the gold left over after paying all the costs.

The strangest thing about this debacle was that the position we were in was the very kind of thing a trader looks out for. "Sell-the-Pig Jim" was perhaps one of the best traders around, known to trade first and ask later. Perhaps it was the "New York Minute Syndrome" because the opportunity could not be explained in less than a minute. Perhaps "The Shark" knew what lay ahead and just wanted his money back. Whatever the stupidity, the deed was done and, once again, I was on my own, trying to salvage my pride and my pocketbook.

There was only one course I could take to recover from what had become for me a life-changing event. I had to find new partners and best the offer on the table within forty-eight hours. I was able to pull off this feat because I had gained the trust of the senior partner of the merchant bank that had financed our new mine in the very recent past. He knew far better than anyone the huge potential of the new gold find and did not hesitate to jump in and better the bid made to "Sell-the-Pig Jim." In this rescue, I was put in a strange position in that I was a seller in the old partnership and a buyer in a new loose group of institutional shareholders.

As required, the commitment was made within forty-eight hours with a closing within five days, leaving "The Shark" buyers in the dust. The effect was immediate once the market realized the traders were gone and new serious investors had stepped up to the plate. It was very much a matter of follow the leader. There is no better buy in the stock market than a successful gold story. Within three months, the price of the company's shares had nearly doubled, netting a tidy profit for the new investors.

Our shares were listed on NASDAQ, the all-electronic US stock exchange, and the stodgy old Toronto exchange, the traditional home of gold mining companies. As our story became accepted, shares flowed to the far larger electronic market in the United States. This would prove to be a good news-bad news situation. Good news on the upside, bad news on the downside. We landed right in the middle of "irrational exuberance," the phrase coined by Alan Greenspan, the erstwhile Chairman of the Federal Reserve, to describe the frenzy of buying in the stock market The stock market crash in October 1987 would prove the bad news of the downside when market makers on the NASDAQ stopped answering their phones. This caused the shares of smaller companies to go into free fall.

Once again it did not seem to make sense for shares of pure gold companies to go into the tank when uncertainty loomed, trumping one of the reasons for buying gold in the first place. But with market makers hiding, the desire for liquidity rained supreme and price lost all relevance. Before it was all over, we would see the value of our small company plunge by seventy-five percent, a figure that was less than the cash we had in the bank and far less than the market value of the gold in our refinery.

But misfortune for one player can very often be opportunity for another. The former was for us, and the latter was for another small gold-miner with lots of ready cash.

* * *

7

' No, no!' said the Queen. 'Sentence first — verdict afterwards.'

–From *Alice's Adventures in Wonderland,* Lewis Carroll

THE LAST HURRAH:

THE RULES OF ENGAGEMENT for takeovers of publicly-listed companies have evolved from regulators over time. They commence with a disclosure requirement when the acquirer, or the fuckor as they are sometimes called, reaches a designated level of ownership of the company under attack, or the fuckee. They then usually require continuous disclosure as more shares are acquired, until a twenty percent threshold is reached when the fuckors must disclose their ultimate intention. As in any war, the rules of engagement are subject to interpretation and a lot of baffle-gab. The words "friendly" and "hostile" are thrown around like chaff, but seldom designate the real purpose behind the purchase. The common statement that the shares are bought "for investment purposes only" has come to mean absolutely zilch. It's all a bit of a joke unless you happen to be an employee of the fuckee and your cozy corporate life is about to come to an abrupt end. The whole process has been high jacked by lawyers and directors under the guise of maximizing returns for shareholders, thereby forcing management to sit on the sidelines and await their fate. Many times it becomes a very public auction process, one that enriches the lawyers and financial advisers more than the investors.

It is assumed, rightly in many cases, that the fuckor is trying to steal from the fuckee. The first line of defense is for the directors of the fuckee to hire a financial advisor, usually a merchant bank or other financial intermediary in order to "maximize value" for the remaining shareholders of the fuckee. In real-speak this means to find another buyer, a White Knight, who will ride to the rescue and pay a higher price, or agree to "Greenmail" (another word for extortion), and buy back the stake held by the fuckor, or agree to a standstill.

Behind all the business-speak lies the real reason for the attempted heist. It can be as simple as blatant opportunism when the price of the fuckee's shares do not reflect the real value of the underlying assets. In the case of a public gold company, this can be an easy calculation since so much information is in the public domain. Once a mine is operating successfully, it does not take rocket science to figure out the incredible leverage that accompanies the value of the shares. If investors own shares in a gold company that has substantial multi-year reserves of gold, they are in effect "long gold" and have a call on the price of gold far into the future. The price or value of gold is incredibly volatile and can increase or decrease by huge amounts in very short periods of time. There are no limits, up or down, on the trading of gold futures in a given trading session, so the long-term approaches offered by shares of producing gold companies are still popular, despite being labeled dinosaurs by the financial elite.

I already had a financial advisor, a merchant bank owned by the very big bank that had sold me the ugly duckling which had suddenly become a white swan. One small problem was that this financial advisor also had our fuckor as a client and therefore had a direct conflict of interest. Making matters even more complicated, the advisor also had as clients the new group of investors, including myself, that had financed the buyout of "The Shark" and promptly seen the value of their investment reduced to a pittance by the stock market crash.

In the financial world, enlightened self-interest frequently comes ahead of worry over possible conflicts of interest. This case would prove no different. We went through the motions, but the issue was never in doubt. We were doing a mating dance with numerous other gold players, some of whom were very helpful, but nothing could stem the tide of share purchases by our fuckor. During this period, the price of our shares was very volatile, jumping all over the place. There were press releases from both sides, but there was no doubt as to who was winning. I spent hours trying to coax my new partners into hanging in there for a higher price, but the memory of the recent crash was all too vivid, and they soon succumbed to the temptation of ready cash over an uncertain future.

My board of directors, all of whom had lots of stock options, were supportive until they were reminded by the lawyers that their imminent dismissal should have no bearing on their deliberations. I was totally pissed off with myself for not having seen this coming. Once we had removed the control held by "The Shark," we were fair game for predators with a sharp eye for emerging situations. The stock market crash had only exacerbated an already prescient situation. It turned out that our fuckor knew a lot more about us than I cared to imagine. The company, although long in ready cash, was in trouble because of labor unrest and falling grades at their main production unit at Red lake in Canada. They also owned a gold property near our mine in the Black Hills and no doubt had in mind a combined operation heavily slanted to their advantage. I had been told by a friend to beware any company run by an accountant and here was a prime example of why I should have paid more heed to his admonition.

In between all the thrashing around, I was now under the gun to resolve my personal finances, in complete disarray since the stock market disaster. It's one thing to be fired from one's occupation with a stash of money. It's quite another to be out in the cold and heavily in debt. The answer appeared out of the blue in a call from a stockbroker friend whose brother was a fellow miner. As it turned out, we owned a class of shares that were indexed to the price of gold while still being convertible to our common shares. Because of the extreme market volatility, the price of the indexed shares had become completely out of whack with our other shares. When this happens it allows for an arbitrage between the two classes of shares. Simply put, arbitrage is making two and two into four, when everyone else says it should be three or five. If the spread is great enough, it can be very profitable over a short period of time, or until other traders figure it out. I figured it out in a big way and, helped by my stockbroker friend, took full advantage. It also proved to be an excellent defensive tactic since it involved the issue of a raft of new common shares in our company, thus making it more expensive for our fuckor to gain the desired degree of control.

This would prove to be my last hurrah, but the huge trade I pulled off made me feel a whole lot better. It would also remind me of the Mark Rich quote that a trader walks on the knife edge so it is best not to step off. I had stepped off and paid the price.

* * *

8

THE BAY STREET BOYS:

THE MERCHANT BANKS OF TORONTO, centered on Bay Street (the Canadian equivalent of Wall Street), became major players in World Mine Finance over a hundred year period that started and ended with mineral discoveries near the town of Timmins in Northern Ontario. To begin with, it was gold, and the discovery made by the mining syndicate of Noah Timmins would become the famous Hollinger Gold Mine, made infamous by the exploits of Conrad Black. In the end, it would be the multi-mineral massive sulfide discovery at Kidd Creek that would bring the curtain down on the longest running crap game in history.

The Bay Street Boys, as they came to be known, were the croupiers who ran the game that would allow a few to become very rich and a great many others to become punters or speculators on the floor and on the streets surrounding the Toronto Stock Exchange. It was like a never-ending gold rush that, with short intermissions for two world wars, saw hundreds of millions of dollars from all over the world pour into the coffers of the dealers and their handlers, the partners of the Merchant Banks.

It might have continued for a lot longer had it not been for the fiasco of Windfall Mines that took place in the summer of 1974. A husband and wife team, who promoted themselves as geologists, were principals in a small public company with the dubious name of Windfall Mines. As luck would have it, Windfall was the proud owner of claims abutting the incredibly rich Kidd Creek Discovery near Timmins. The early betting was the chances were slim; the riches of Kidd Creek extended under the Windfall Claims. Undeterred and backed by the dealers of Bay Street, the Windfall Duo commenced core drilling to probe deep into the ground near its border with the Kidd Creek property.

For some then inexplicable reason, the results of the drilling were kept secret. When inquiries were made, media outlets received anonymous telegrams containing bogus results that whipped the trading of Windfall shares into a frenzy, driving up the price of the shares by 500%. Millions of dollars were made and lost before the truth emerged: the assays from the drilling contained nothing of value.

In a fit of pique, apparently because so many small investors had been duped, Provincial politicians were forced to shut down the gaming table and drove the traders out of town to a new location in far away Vancouver, British Columbia. Truth be known, there was nothing really new about all of this. The dealers had merely broken the eleventh commandment by getting caught. Manipulating the prices of shares of small public mining companies had been common practice for nearly a hundred years. It had become a fine art during the Cold War when the demand for uranium and nickel found in safe places such as the Great Canadian Shield drove the markets for exploration companies to levels never before seen.

An entrepreneur will typically look for a commodity that everyone wants and is prepared to pay a lot of money for. This is the easy part. Much harder is the task of actually finding a deposit on which to trade.

Perhaps the best known example of such a wheeler-dealer was Joseph Hirschhorn, a Latvian immigrant from the US, more specifically from Wall Street

Joe escaped the debacle of 1929 through shrewd dealing and came to Canada at the height of the Great Depression, carrying with him the then-unthinkable sum of $4 million. He was looking for gold, but would later settle for Uranium (the new gold). He did not know how to go about it, but he soon found out after his famous advertisement in a mining journal, "My name is opportunity and I am calling Canada," produced a flood of possibilities.

Joe was, first and foremost, a stockbroker, and a very shrewd one at that. Experience gained on Wall Street was essential to his mode of operation, which was to never put all your eggs in one basket and to never tell anyone exactly what you owned or, just as important, how you owned it. These traits would make him very rich but also land him in a lot of trouble with regulators.

Joe met up with a clever geologist, Frank Jubin, who pitched him the theory of a giant Uranium deposit in Northern Ontario, later dubbed the "Big Z." It's pretty certain Joe knew little or nothing about the theory, but he knew a great deal about the art of promotion, and how to use old-fashioned greed to raise a lot of money. Using Jubin as the front man to raise the high-risk funds for drilling, and no doubt to take the fall if the results did not prove out, he manipulated the ownership of the claims into a myriad of small, publicly listed exploration companies in which he owned secret interests. As the drill results began to prove Jubin's theory, he traded shares in these companies so as to increase his ownership at the expense of the punters who played the game of chance on the Toronto Stock Exchange.

When the time came to cash in his chips, Joe's acumen as a dealer once again came to the fore. He sold out to mineral conglomerate Rio Tinto, and agent of the British Government charged with acquiring a secure source of Uranium for the production of Nuclear Weapons. It was left to these stalwarts to sort out "the whole ball of shit," as Joe called it, by consolidating all the interests into one entity so as to actually produce the Uranium.

Hounded by regulators for various crimes, Joe became a Landed Immigrant in Canada, and then promptly fled back to the US where he donated his art collection to Uncle Sam in return for respectability. A gallery in DC still bears his name.

Others, who aped his modus operandi while receiving the credit for finding major mineral deposits, followed. Just how well accepted their shady dealings were is evidenced by the fact that Joe and two of his protégés are members of the Canadian Mining Hall of Fame.

In the days before electronic trading, when traders on the floor of the Exchange actually faced off and traded shares, there were many tricks for manipulating the price of shares. "Wash trading", a practice of trading shares between secretly associated owners so as to attract buyers, was an everyday occurrence that was seldom punished. A more complicated scheme involved trading from the "Box," or "Pump and Dump" as its was sometimes referred to. Here, promoters hid the ownership of a control position in the listed shares of a company so as to control the trade and the price of he shares. If successful, this practice could lead to selling new shares at a higher price and avoiding dilution to the promoters.

In the good old days, news traveled relatively slowly, allowing traders to position themselves in the shares of a company ahead of the release of the news. This practice, now called "front running," was very common and often lead to uncontrolled mayhem on the floor of the Exchange, sometimes extending to the sidewalks, or "Curb," outside the Exchange.

Regulators tried in vain to control the mayhem, but before governments discovered lotteries, there was an insatiable demand for what was, in reality, legalized gambling. There was a constant drumbeat from prospectors and mine promoters who relied on the dealers to raise the high-risk funds used for mine exploration. A clever promoter could make a great deal of money for a dealer and vice versa. Sometimes, amongst all the hype and noise, someone would even find something of real value.

When a meaningful discovery was made, a different dynamic took over. A speculator had little interest in awaiting the slow, tedious work of determining whether a mineral deposit was economic, or for the even longer wait for possible dividends. So the speculators would sell their shares in order to move onto the next "hot" bet, and long-term investors interested in actually owning gold would buy—a process that frequently led to lower share values and a change in controlling ownership. Nowhere was this dichotomy more apparent than with gold discoveries.

When public companies were first used to finance the search for gold, founders and prospectors—some of whom would become Gold Barons—had discovered a neat trick of issuing two kinds of shares so as hang onto control of whatever gold might be produced. The ruse was selling a few "super shares" with the power of multiple votes to the founders and their families and friends, while selling lots of regular shares to the great-unwashed public. It was well-accepted by the Bay Street Boys for promoters to control gold mines by this method, provided the rewards continued to flow into the right hands.

Over time, some of these "super companies" would become very valuable for purposes other than mining gold. In the hands of astute financiers, they could be used for control of vast wealth and personal enrichment. They could also be used to seize control of other gold companies. In 1987, two of these super gold companies would commence battle for control of large amounts of gold in the Black Hills.

For hundreds of years, gold was a super currency riding above the fray of uncertainty and devaluation as a safe haven for investors and traders alike. It still might be, despite the claims of central bankers who view it as a nuisance factor, if the problem of liquidity could be overcome. Gold keeps its value because it is very rare and, to date, no one has found a way to destroy or duplicate the metal. Most of the world's supply of gold is locked away in vaults and cannot be used as a means of satisfying financial obligations undertaken in trade. That is, unless a way is found to link the currency of trade directly to a fixed amount of gold. This was the idea of the Bank of England on Threadneedle Street in the Old City of London, an institution that successfully ruled worldwide trade for over one hundred years.

The step back toward the era of the Gold Standard would occur toward the end of the twentieth century when, after years of fierce lobbying by the Word Gold Council, regulators in New York, London and Toronto allowed the issuance of Exchange Traded Funds, making certain shares exchangeable for a fixed amount of gold. The idea for such an instrument originated from a little-known gold mining company and a famous Toronto Merchant Bank as a means of financing a gold mine in the Black Hills. The concept for this financial instrument was simple: if the gold-miner had the physical gold, it could meet the agreed terms of any type of exchange. A simple concept, but the devil lay in the details.

* * *

HEMLO – THE GREENSTONE MONSTER:

HEMLO IS THE STORY OF A HUGE GOLD DEPOSIT discovered in 1980 by a clever geologist who, after thirty-five years of futile efforts by his peers, was able to unlock the mystery of the greenstone porphyry rock and, in so doing, instigate the last great gold rush of the twentieth century. The deposit was named after a small hamlet on the rugged North Shore of Lake Ontario, a long way from any civilization. Like much of the great Canadian Shield, the area was first explored by surveyors for the Canadian Pacific Railway looking for a passage through the swamp and rock-strewn terrain. It would be the same railway that would bring the prospectors following gold discoveries near Timmins in the late nineteenth century.

Finding gold in the great batholiths of the Canadian Shield was very different from the traditional method of panning in rivers and streams. The rocks were more than a billion years old and had been scraped by glaciers through numerous ice ages, so very little gold that might have been present remained near the surface. In the nineteenth century, rotary drills capable of recovering cores had not been invented, and so explorers were forced to excavate shafts to determine if gold was present below the surface, an arduous process that would deter all but the most zealous of gold enthusiasts.

Hemlo differed from the norm because the area contained numerous gold showings at, or very near the surface, a happenstance that attracted a Canadian prospector by the name of Jack Williams. Williams was a quiet and dogged individual who played his cards very close to his chest. Working alone through numerous summers, he managed to produce a body of work, which demonstrated that the gold was contained in a porphyry rock not dissimilar to that present at the prodigious Lake Shore Gold Mine that had started the Ontario Gold Rush of the nineteenth century. Williams went on to publish his findings and be granted patented ownership of the claims he had staked and explored.

The process of patenting granted him and his heir's title to all gold and precious metals that lay under the claims. It also assured that anyone wishing to mine there would have to enter into a lease agreement and pay a royalty based on the market value of all minerals recovered. If Williams had known what riches lay a few hundred feet under the surface, he might have tried to attract a financier in the form of another mining company, but with no evidence of high-grade gold, he was forced to rely on others to generate the necessary excitement. By design, the patenting of claims attracts a crowd, and Hemlo was no different. Several companies staked and drilled a large surrounding area, but the results were inconclusive and the claims were allowed to lapse, leaving racks of drill cores showing small amounts of gold in a green colored porphyry rock.

As gold prices rose in the 1970's to never-before-seen levels, interest in the area was re-awakened, and three prospectors gathered up all the published information, re-staked the properties in their own names, and tried without success to find a partner to finance additional drilling. The Toronto Stock Market for junior mining companies lay in ruins after the Windfall Mines caper, so the three amigos turned to the Vancouver Stock Market for help. They leased their newly staked properties to a very small mining exploration company financed by a manic stock promoter who knew little to nothing about gold. Luckily, the promise of funding once again trumped uncertainty, and the prospectors managed to retain the services of a very clever British geologist who knew a great deal about gold.

David Bell was a different kind of geologist in that he was articulate, patient, and knew what he was doing. He determined that the greenstone was in reality a volcanic intrusive that was squeezed between very old rocks found in the Canadian Shield and the younger sedimentary rocks found under the Great Lakes. As such, there could well be more gold at depth than that showing close to the surface. He also warned his employers that the heart of the big Greenstone deposit could very well lie under the adjacent Williams' claims and recommended that a lease be concluded with the owners.

Exploring for gold is at best a huge gamble and at worst a foolhardy exercise in futility. There are few rules and many ways to screw up, one of which is to brag to the world about a gold strike before acquiring or leasing all the claims that surround the discovery. It is almost impossible to secure any form of ownership after the cat is out of the bag. Unbelievably, this is what happened in the case of the small, inexperienced explorer at Hemlo. The prospector Williams had gone on to his reward, leaving a widow who could not be found. Meanwhile, the drills were turning and the money needed to keep the exploration camp going was running out. So it was decided to bring in a mining partner to help finance the ongoing program.

There were lots to see and hear from a geologist who appeared to have solved the conundrum of the Hemlo Gold, and many large gold mining companies were keen to talk about a possible joint venture. In a display of reckless abandon, or plain stupidity, the growing data bank of drill results was shown to Lac Minerals, a gold mining company well-known for cut-throat dealing and dishonesty, without first obtaining the normal confidentiality and non-compete agreements. The exploration team went further and suggested the vital importance of the Williams property in various development scenarios. It was as if the lunatics were loose in the asylum when a further fateful decision was made to keep the drills operating while discussions with the rogue Lac continued. Shortly thereafter, the final piece of the puzzle fell into place: the core from the seventy-second drill hole revealed the presence of high-grade gold. This ignited the fires of gold fever and set in motion the Greenstone or Hemlo Gold Rush.

Greenstone was the first gold rush in the electronic age, and the first ever to be driven by a single individual, who we shall call "The Pez." He had, to this point, raised all the money for the current exploration program. Now this same "Pez" became a business magnet by agreeing to raise money for a host of small companies all promising to find the green porphyry rock that hosted the Hemlo gold.

Small wonder he did not have the time to focus on what was going on in the Hemlo camp. His behavior would change in a heartbeat when it became known that Lac, with whom he envisioned a joint venture, had agreed with the widow Williams to lease the patented mining claims, so vital to his project, and to place the property into production for their own account. It was as if the gold so hard won had been stolen from under his very nose. The magnitude of the theft, only to become apparent much later, was at least seven million ounces of gold with a then-current value of over two billion dollars.

To the uninitiated, the scale of this larceny might seem unreal but it was not. The history of gold discoveries is full of stories of opportunistic financiers robbing prospectors of their rightful due. It seemed this kind of behavior was to be expected as the norm in the gold mining business.

For the first time, the project now received the undivided attention of promoters and managers alike. In a burst of frantic activity, battle was joined with Lac to recover the stolen gold. Lac was about to discover there is nothing more dangerous than a scorned stock promoter with a giant ego. In a further timely move, John May, a very successful dealmaker, gave support to the group and a joint venture agreement with an experienced mining company was concluded. The new agreement would see the property placed into production and, in one of the most prescient of decisions, provide funding for a legal action to recover the Williams' claims.

The decision to launch an expensive and drawn-out lawsuit was fraught with risk. The facts were not at issue; the small mining company had been royally screwed by a much bigger rival and the stakes were enormous. In the absence of written contracts, any ruling would depend on the word of the participants—always a toss up.

The law itself was at issue. Would a judge in a civil action be wiling to find a breach of trust where the defendant would claim his actions were simply the normal course of business for the mining industry? And what of the possible remedies? By judgment day, there would likely be two mines producing gold from the same formation on adjacent properties with different operators, making any accounting problematic.

The stock market was quick to express the judgment of the punters and the early betting gave the advantage to the defendant, a spread that would increase during the litigation. But the punters were wrong, and Hemlo would once again surprise. The trial judge ruled in favor of the under-dog and, as an unprecedented remedy, stipulated the mine built on the Williams' property, along with all of the gold, be returned to the plaintiffs.

This judgment would survive appeals to the highest court in the land and it changed the conduct of the mining business forever. Henceforth, business and morality would not be mutually exclusive domains, and negotiating parties would have to accept a fiduciary obligation to act in an ethical manner between each other, even in the absence of written contracts.

This was no slap on the wrist for Lac, and the consequences of the remedy would prove prohibitively expensive to those involved. For not long thereafter, the company would be sold to a larger rival for a fraction of its former value.

As for the Greenstone Monster, the Hemlo formation would produce, over the life of three mines, more than twenty-two million ounces of gold, rendering it the largest gold producer in North America. The junior mining company, after a few years in the sun, frittered away its riches without finding anything else of value. And, despite expenditures of millions of dollars over many years, no one has yet found another gold bearing Greenstone.

* * *

10

THE FIX AND PROBLEMS FOR BARRICK GOLD:

THE LONDON "FIX" is the method by which the World Gold Price is determined. Officially the "Fix" is the average price, expressed in various currencies, of warrants representing pure gold bars traded by five banks in London in morning and afternoon trading sessions.

The practice of the "Fix," or fixing, was started at the conclusion of the First World War by N. M Rothschild, banker to the British Crown since the days of the Napoleonic Wars. The need for a daily system of valuing gold arose when the Gold Standard, which involved an implied guarantee of a fixed ratio between gold and Sterling for over a hundred years, was abandoned by the British government in favor of a floating exchange rate for gold with no implied guarantees by the Bank of England.

There was just not enough gold in the vaults of the Nation to pay for the huge debts run up by Britain and its allies to fight the First World War. The official explanation provided by the bankers was the need for liquidity; the unofficial reason was that the Crown was bankrupt and could no longer sustain a guarantee for the value of Sterling. At the time, London was still the center of world trade, and a published fix would give comfort to those that accepted the currency as a medium of exchange and a store of value. Over time, the American dollar, backed by a huge hoard of gold in Fort Knox, would replace Sterling as the currency of choice for international trade. With the system of fixed exchange rates then in use by the industrialized nations, the relevance and implied guarantee of gold remained.

In 1972, then-President Nixon, facing imminent rampant inflation, repeated the actions of the British in 1917 and cut the fixed ratio between gold and the American dollar. The official explanation was once again the need for liquidity in the face of floating exchange rates then promulgated by the trading nations of the Western Powers. The unofficial reason was that there was not enough gold to cover the huge increases in the money supply made necessary by the funding of America's continued wars.

Despite modern-day economic theory, which would like to forget about gold, it is still accepted as an official reserve currency by the International Monetary Fund, and the London Bullion Market is the widely accepted market for central banks to buy and sell gold reserves. It remains a very small and volatile market run by only five banks, but its daily "fixes" are still watched by traders all over the world.

Like many other commodities, spot prices for gold follow the sun from East to West and form the benchmarks for gold futures trading on the COMEX in New York, as well as many other commodity exchanges in Asia. It was on COMEX that the battle between the World Gold Council (the ruling association of gold producers) and the world's largest producer of gold was fought. This was a contest that would determine how gold was valued in the future.

After the stagflation suffered by the western industrial nations in the 1970's, gold prices peaked at never before seen levels, and gold producers became the kings of the heap for investors scared to death of further inflation and currency devaluation. It was a heady time for the princes that ran the large gold producers, since their shares were treated by the investment community as a form of currency that could be used to buy almost anything. One such prince was fed the idea that the good times could last forever if he would contract to sell at a fixed price some or all of the company's gold still in the ground by way of futures contracts on COMEX. In the vernacular of the trader, these were called short sales because the seller did not have the pure gold at the time of the forward sale contract but did have the ability or the credit to deliver the gold if required on the termination of the contract.

The purpose of this form of financial engineering was to transfer the risk from the gold producer to the buyers of the forward contracts. In theory, this would convert a risky gold producer into a form of bank with almost limitless credit to buy other gold producers or any other form of investment that could promise to hold its value during periods of inflation. In a coup-De-grace, the accountants and auditors were bamboozled into agreeing that there would be no recorded losses on the books of the company from these contracts. Forward contracts showing losses on their expiry date would be rolled over to a future date, thus deferring any possible loss. In the meantime, profits would be piled up, and shareholders would get much richer than they would watching their company mine gold.

It was a dream proposition for a man with a giant ego hell bent on building the biggest gold company in the world. Known as "The Monk" to gold miners he was the president and founder of a gold company that discovered the mother load of gold deposits in the wastelands of Nevada. He also had a history as a clever promoter with a less-than-stellar record of success, a trait that would serve him well in the rough and tumble of the gold business.

"The Monk" would become the prophet of the voodoo mathematics involved in persuading investors that falling gold values were good for gold producers, a proposition at odds with the historic reasons for owning shares in gold companies as a safe haven from inflation. The trick was to promise investors that it was possible to have the proverbial cake and eat it at the same time. Meanwhile, the main business of the company remained the same, namely that of putting the rock in the box everyday at the cheapest possible cost, leaving the accounting to the wizards in the head office.

At the outset, the scheme worked better than "The Monk" could have hoped. Gold prices were falling, as were the share prices for other gold producers, leaving them ripe for acquisition. And acquire he did, quickly bulking up his company and catching up to the then-largest gold producer also based in Nevada.

The apparent competitive advantage offered by hedging, as forward selling was called, attracted the attention of other producers including the South African giant Goldfields. Producers became divided between those that hedged their production and those led by Goldfields who considered the practice at odds with the long-term objectives of the gold industry.

Goldfields were a founding member of the World Gold Council, the association of gold producers dedicated to promoting the use of gold. The Council was working to gain acceptance by regulatory authorities for a new form of security that would allow buyers to hedge the "long side" of the market, as opposed to the "short side" advocated by "The Monk" and his followers. This would be accomplished by causing the World Gold Council to do what the Bank of England had done during the one hundred years of the Gold Standard: guarantee the delivery of gold required to link the new securities to a fixed amount of gold. In this manner, investors could hedge against the possibility of inflation without the expense of owning the metal.

It was a brilliant idea that would attract new investment into the industry and limit the supply of gold available, as the physical metal was purchased by the investment funds offering the new gold-linked securities. It would also illustrate the classic dichotomy between the opposing sides of the market.

The battle was joined when security regulators in London and New York approved the sale of Exchange Traded Funds backed by gold. Almost immediately, gold prices were turned on their ear, and "The Monk" and his company were trapped in a brutal short squeeze. As gold prices rose so did the cash cost of rolling over the gold short sales, as marginal calls came from the brokers who had written the contracts that dated all the way back to the beginning of the charade.

Worse was the reaction of Wall Street, where analysts were quick to realize the conundrum facing the company. The more gold prices went up the more acute the problem became. Now the price of the company's shares was stuck while the value of their competitor's shares increased: exactly the opposite of the situation that had allowed "The Monk" and his cohorts to gobble up so many of their competitors.

The agony would continue with management changes and denial of the fact that the problem originated at the very top of organization and a sympathetic and well paid Board of Directors, all friends of "The Monk" How else to explain the suicidal risks taken by the Company in shorting gold, in a market with no limits and a long history of extreme volatility.

The eventual price of this insanity would round out to 3.5 billion dollars a sum greater than the entire net worth of the company.

* * *

11

All that glitters is not gold
— Proverb, Unknown

THE SEARCH FOR GOLD IN THE JUNGLES OF BORNEO:

THE PROCESS OF EXPLORING FOR GOLD can be likened to looking for a very small needle in a giant haystack. Making the process even harder is the likelihood that many times the gold is invisible to the naked eye, leaving possible discovery in the hands of metallurgists performing fire assays or other forms of chemical analysis. There are all kinds of tools available to geologists to determine where gold might be found but only one method of confirming the actual presence of gold. This is by drilling and analyzing the rock chips or cores taken from drill holes. It is an extremely exacting process that requires careful sampling and sophisticated laboratories that are seldom, if ever, near where the drilling is being conducted.

"Salting" is slang for a process that involves tampering with crushed samples of rock by sprinkling minute grains of gold into the mix so as to inflate results obtained by fire assays. It is a practice that has fallen out of favor since it was used to perpetuate the largest mining fraud ever attempted. There are many stories about crime mysteries that are ultimately solved. There are far fewer stories of crimes that remain unsolved and fewer still of crimes that remain unsolved by virtue of cover-up or neglect. The latter best describes the bizarre case of Busang, the six million dollar fraud involving imaginary gold in the jungles of Borneo.

In March 1996, a forty-one-year-old Filipino geologist working for a Canadian junior mining company apparently jumped to his death from a helicopter taking him to an exploration camp near the town of Samarinda deep in the Borneo jungle. Two days later, it was reported that a rambling seven-page letter found by local police confirmed suicide under very strange circumstances. This husband to at least three wives and benefactor to countless girlfriends was returning from a trip to far away Toronto where he had received the accolades of his peers for the apparent discovery of a giant gold deposit. He had been summoned to answer the rather delicate question of why an audit of drill results taken from the discovery holes showed that no gold was present, despite the glowing results previously published, which had led to stock market valuation of six-billion dollars.

It had all begun three years before this fateful day when a small company listed on the Alberta Stock Exchange made an arrangement with a Dutch-Canadian geologist, who we will call John, to drill a potential gold property on the Island of Borneo in South East Asia. The small company was managed by an unsuccessful stockbroker, who we will call David, and his wife who were desperate for a project to save their company. No doubt they were deemed suitable because they knew nothing about exploration for gold and would not question what was going on in a far-away exploration camp. John, who claimed to have been a discoverer of the famous Octedi copper-and-gold deposit in Indonesia, was also desperate for a winner to stoke his immense ego. He also needed to justify to an Australian investor a previous promotion of a potential gold property that had failed to live up to his rosy projections.

The property had the right address in that it was situated on the Ring of Fire, home to some of the most prolific gold and copper deposits in the world. The area was of particular interest because itinerant unlicensed prospectors were panning alluvial gold from nearby rivers. It was this source of small, rounded flakes of gold that would be critical to the great ruse that was about to commence.

David borrowed money from a friend and flew to Jakarta to meet with John and his assistant, a Filipino geologist who had experience working in Borneo. The details of the meeting are murky, but the results speak for themselves. A deal was concluded that must have seemed like a dream-come-true for John and his wife: the little Alberta company would be granted the right to drill the "hot" property in return for a commitment of two million dollars. In a very unusual twist, the geologists agreed to help fund the drill program by bringing investors they knew to the table. They would also obtain the necessary permits and organize the infrastructure required to transport and test drill core at the nearby town of Samarinda. For all intents and purposes, all that the stockbroker was bringing to the table was a public shell-company listed on the regional stock exchange. To anyone but a desperate idiot, this would have seemed too good to be true, but the possibility of financial salvation won out over prudence, and financing to raise the money proceeded.

There were two methods open to the Alberta company to raise the money required to drill the property. One involved the issuance of a prospectus approved by regulators. The other, far more expeditious method involved a private placement to select investors without all the fuss and expense involved in public perusal. The company went the down-and-dirty route of a private placement and raised the two million dollars by issuing shares at a price of fifty cents per share to relatively few buyers, many of whom were nominees for the real owners. Apparently, the Indonesian geologists were good on their word, and the share-issue closed without any difficulty. Shortly thereafter, drilling at Busang commenced.

Exploring for gold is an intricate business where a matter of inches can determine whether gold is present in the host rock being drilled. Drilled core is returned to the surface in a core barrel where it is logged by a geologist who makes copious notes on the appearance of rock formations that may contain gold. The core is then split down the middle lengthwise and one half is bagged-and-tagged for transport to the laboratory where it is crushed, sampled, and fire-tested for the presence of even minute quantities of gold. The remaining half of the core is stored and kept for confirmation testing, if required. It is an almost unheard-of and extremely dubious practice for the whole core to be sent for testing and not be available for further analysis. Yet this is what transpired from the very first hole drilled in the property at Busang. Whole sections of core were bagged and shipped by barge down the Busang River to a laboratory at Samarinda. On the way, the bags were opened and the contents sprinkled with gold dust so as to assure positive results.

The continuation of the salting operation was no simple matter because it involved the cooperation of several people who knew how and where to add the alluvial gold flakes to the samples. Over time, the sheer volume of samples being barged down the river must have kept a small army of helpers busy. The helpers and the geologists knew what they were doing was illegal, and that if they were caught they could face Indonesian justice—not a heartwarming thought at the best of times. The only plausible explanation was that they were being handsomely rewarded by outside sources, sufficiently enough to compensate for the loss of their livelihood if they were exposed. The outside source could only have been someone who was well-acquainted with the whole scheme and who'd had the opportunity from the very beginning to recoup the added costs by selling large numbers of shares of the Alberta company at a profit.

It is not a wild stretch of the imagination to surmise that the perpetrators of this scheme could be found in the buyers of the original private placement of the small company's shares. The more problematic question is why this operation remained undetected for nearly three years. Historically, salting operations would be limited so as to inflate the shares of the company carrying out the drilling for a short time. Once the perpetrators had made their score, the imaginary gold would disappear and everyone would walk away, giving the appearance of just another unsuccessful attempt to find gold. In this case, the process was manageable, since the Alberta company was run by an idiot who was so enamored of having a success story for the first time in his life that he would do almost anything to keep the price of the company's shares rising.

Funding the expanding Busang camp was another matter, one that would soon involve some major international banks and their advisors, not the least of which were mining analysts who certainly should have been able to spot the glaring inconsistencies and questionable mining practices involved.

When gold is first discovered in a rock formation, it is critical to determine very early on if the gold can be recovered by conventional means at a reasonable cost. This involves metallurgical testing and microscopic analysis of drill cores by experts. Had such tests been performed, they would have shown that the gold in the samples was alluvial in origin and no doubt sourced from nearby rivers, as opposed to being part of a chemical rock matrix as would have been expected.

Over a period of two and a half years, over sixty million dollars would be raised by selling shares at ever increasing prices to professional fund managers and investors without so much as a single question being raised as to the authenticity of the results or the competence of the managers. Worse it seems was the report commissioned by John and prepared by a well-respected engineering consulting firm that confirmed a possible resource of over one hundred million ounces of gold. Small wonder that the wild promotion ran amok and the price of the company's shares soared over four thousand percent to the unthinkable price of two hundred dollars a share.

The end did not originate with the financiers or the consultants but with the greedy brother of the ruling Indonesian despot. He demanded a piece of the imaginary deposit for his family, using the threat of withholding permits required for mine development as a club. For the first time, this seemingly administrative matter focused attention on the fact that the small Alberta company was incapable of managing the huge project without direction from mining experts and a knowledgeable board of directors.

It would be a board member who would first seriously question the antics of John, who had now moved to the Cayman Islands so as shield his stock dealings from the eyes of regulators and the grasp of the tax man. David, who had set up shop in the tax haven of Nassau, was now forced to seek a partnership with a major mining company as a way to bring a degree of sanity and order to a situation that had obviously spun out of control.

There was now no doubt that the great fraud would be exposed, and everyone should have been scared, but it was too late. The process hurtled to its inevitable end when confirmation drilling found no gold. Predictably, the shares of what was once the darling of investors quickly became worthless, despite assurances from John that there really was a gold deposit on the property. Everyone else involved took cover. The board of directors commissioned a report by a well-respected mining engineer, the minor perpetrators who had salted the drill core fled into the jungle, the Indonesian government promised swift retribution and did nothing, and a criminal investigation was launched in North America to appease the irate small investors who took the brunt of the losses.

Befitting this tale of greed, the ultimate ending was as strange as the beginning. David never lived to enjoy his stock market coup and died from a stroke shortly thereafter. John was placed under house arrest in the Cayman Islands and was forced to spend his rewards on a protracted six-year successful legal battle against charges of insider trading. The Board of Directors received a report confirming the giant fraud while exonerating themselves. The Indonesians quickly gave up in the face of pressure from the ruling family. The criminal investigators came as close as anyone to unraveling the apparent mystery before being shut down, maybe because they had come all too close to exposing gross negligence by some of the very powerful financial institutions involved.

The answer to the puzzle lay at the beginning rather than the end of the story. There can be little doubt that the rest off the perpetrators were to be found amongst the original investors. These were the people who planned and financed a charade that was only meant to last a matter of months rather than years. Their mistake was in underestimating the greed of the actors charged with carrying out the deed and the possibility of those actors carrying on a fraud long after it became certain that it would be discovered.

* * *

12

KING COAL AND THE MAN THAT NEVER WAS:

THE STRANGEST MINING STORY I ever came across involved Metallurgical Coal.

I am able to relate this tale because for a short while I ran a coal mining company situated in the Crows Nest Pass in South Western Alberta at the behest of a large Canadian energy company that had made a hasty and disastrous foray into the business.

The Crows Nest Pass was famous for its coal mines, and at one point in history was home to a very large population of relatively well-paid coal miners who were willing to take on the horrifying risks of toiling in dangerous underground mines. But by the end of the Second World War, the boom was over as the boilers of the railway steam locomotives were converted from coal to oil and most mines were shut down.

At about this time, a clever entrepreneur by the name of Frank Harquail began acquiring the shares of coal-mining companies that nobody else wanted. These companies owned vast quantities of freehold coal reserves, coal that was suitable for coking. The centerpiece of his new prize was a private company, Hillcrest Collieries, secretly owned by the senior managers of the all-powerful CPR Railway, which also had the dubious distinction of hosting the largest mining disaster in Canadian history.

It is almost impossible to believe that Frank took such a giant leap of faith without some prior inkling of the nascent demand for Coking Coal from the Japanese Steel Mills. General Douglas MacArthur had seen to it that the steel mills were rebuilt after the end of the war, but he could do nothing to replace the existing coalmines that were fast depleting.

The idea of using Coking Coal from Western Canada in Japanese mills was fraught with difficulties. The mines were 700 miles from the nearest port in Vancouver, a port that was designed for wheat not coal. The rail journey required passage over mountainous terrain with fierce winter conditions and it was thought unlikely that the railways would make the required improvements without a real incentive of high freight rates.

The giant trading companies of Japan, who had been tasked with the vital role of feeding the new Japanese juggernaut, thought quite differently and began to encourage a new industry through the promise of long-term contracts.

So began the lonely quest of a man with an iron will to succeed at a seemingly impossible dream. He acquired control of Coleman Collieries, a company that was already producing coking coal for a plant in nearby British Columbia, and was able to convince trading giant Marubeni that he could raise the capital to mechanize the mines and treatment plant. Along the way, Frank got a big boost when the Kaiser family, already heavily involved with steel, began development of the Sparwood property in South East British Columbia after obtaining the promise of a very large long-term contract from Japanese mills.

The expected bonanza was slow to commence because agreed-to prices at the West Coast Port bore no resemblance to the realities faced by the new mines or the railway. Young Edgar Kaiser, keen to earn his spurs in the family business, had assumed costs based upon dragline operations in the Western United States, a totally unrealistic scenario in the high Rocky Mountains. Frank knew better but could do little to improve his situation, and so profits remained illusory while his health deteriorated.

Imagine, then, the jubilation when out of nowhere there appeared a large energy company with a mandate to acquire a coal operation. Price did not appear to be a problem, and soon an army of consultants (some of whom knew nothing about mining coal) was dispatched to conduct due diligence.

It is at this point that this Horatio Alger-like story becomes bizarre. Frank must have had a visceral dislike for paying any form of taxation. He lived in Las Vegas, a no-tax state, and ran his private business from the tax haven of Lyford Key in the Bahamas. Very soon a great deal of cash changed hands and Frank quite literally disappeared from the face of the earth.

Within a year it became apparent that Frank's dream was not all it had appeared to be. His lieutenants had handled the truth very recklessly when they failed to tell the consultants that a large part of the coal reserves could not be recovered by traditional means, thus rendering the price paid by the energy company unrealistic.

After a long and arduous lawsuit, a high court found that malfeasance had indeed occurred and awarded damages that almost equaled the entire purchase price.

Meanwhile, it became known that Frank had died in very unusual circumstances. He had chartered a large private yacht and sailed, on his deathbed, out into the Aegean Sea, where according to his wishes, he was buried at sea. He also died intestate (without a will) leaving all but his widow to doubt that he had ever existed.

It is befitting this strange tale have a happy ending. Frank's widow, Helen, then living on the tax haven of Grand Cayman, returned the judgment money (even though it would never have been found) and went on to become a great benefactor to the Island, using millions of dollars received from the sale of Frank's other coal properties in Western Canada.

* * *

13

MARATHON MEN AND THE CARTAWAY CAPER:

THE STORY OF CARTAWAY has all the baggage typical of a standard micro-cap venture company. It also has a human side that shows us how the business of raising high risk venture capital worked during one of the halcyon periods of mining exploration in Canada.

It seems as though major discoveries of mineral deposits happen about once every ten years, periods of great excitement followed by busts and recriminations for all the wrongs committed by those chasing the dream of untold riches. One such period started in the early 1990's when a small company, Diamond Fields, promoted and financed by Robert Freidland, made the discovery of the huge Voissey Bay nickel deposit in Labrador.

Typical to the norm in the speculative exploration business, both company and promoter had recently been resurrected from the dead. Following his public and nasty scrap with the Environmental Protection Agency in the United States over the Summitville Heap Leech Gold Mine, Robert had moved to Singapore and recommenced his magic. He acquired control of Diamond Fields, a defunct Arkansas company that had fallen on hard times. Diamonds were "hot" at the time, but as luck would have it, they discovered a major nickel deposit instead.

Mining promoters are strange beasts and good ones are rare indeed. Masonic is one way of describing Robert, who has to be one of the greatest promoters ever to appear on the mining scene. With absolutely no background or training in the science of finding mineral deposits, he took to the business like a duck to water. He also had the innate good sense to hire very qualified people who could explain to him what was going on and help him raise the millions required to keep chasing the dream. It is often forgotten that his first and disastrous attempt at the mining business, a small company aptly-named Galactic, had been supported and financed by international engineering giant Bechtel and the Bank of America.

The best friends a mining promoter has are the legions of stock salespeople who toil in the second echelon of Mine Finance, the folks who raise the high-risk capital required to go hunting for mineral elephants, and get very rich in the process. It is very much a two-way street where a good promoter can make a big difference in the outcome.

Once such group of super-salesman came in the form of an upstart security dealer by the name of First Marathon. No dummies, these guys had figured out a new business model to serve the mineral exploration industry. Rather than simply sell shares in exploration companies to individuals, they would own a piece of (or control) the company raising the money. In a further stroke of genius, they would also own captive mutual funds to gobble up the sales product. If this idea worked, and it did beyond their wildest dreams, they would control both the demand and supply sides of the equation, a sure recipe for nirvana.

Cartaway, as the name might imply, was a micro-cap company with shares listed on the Alberta Stock Exchange that had started life leasing garbage containers to the good citizens of Kamloops, BC. Apparently, the garbage business did not go according to plan, and the company had ended up with a share listing but no business, a prime target for the young lions at First Marathon.

A group of brokers in the Calgary and Vancouver offices acquired forty-six percent of the issued shares of Cartaway from the founders for ten cents a share. Before the ink was dry, they then sold another trench of treasury shares to family and friends at a price of twelve cents a share, using the proceeds from this sale to launch the company into the mineral exploration business in a big way.

The Young Lions then, as if by magic, acquired mining claims very close to Voissey Bay controlled by their confidant Robert Freidland. They started work in preparation for a drill program the following summer. At this point, the operation was under control and making a paper profit for the syndicate. With tight control of the "Box," the number of shares issued, every single announcement resulted in further price appreciation, and so everyone was happy. But the company lacked a head liar, a leader who could add luster and bring in the investment dollars needed to fund the exploratory drilling.

The choice for such a leader was John Ivany, a seasoned mining professional with an excellent reputation. John may have known mining as practiced by large companies, but he was totally unprepared for the rough and tumble world of the "juniors" a world wherein the lofty expectations of stock-pushers ruled the day and where a chance remark could result in a surge of trading as nervous punters traded on speculation alone. It was very likely that a remark to the effect that the drill core contained high concentrations of sulfides associated with the Voissey Bay deposit, which had started the trading frenzy in the first place, would also bring the house of cards down.

The resulting stock Market action took everyone by surprise. The limited "float" as designed by the young lions suddenly became a liability as the price of the Cartaway shares soared out of control, attracting the unwanted attention of regulators. It scared the members of the Calgary Office enough to break ranks and dump their shares, all of this before the assay results from the drill core was known. The Genie was now out of the bottle, and the best-laid plans of the perpetrators went up in smoke.

When the assay results became available they confirmed what professionals suspected: the Voissey Bay Formation, hyped by the best mining promoter on the planet, was not present under the Cartaway Claims. And so the stock price crashed back to earth and the game was over.

Unfortunately for those directly involved the story did not end well. Embarrassed regulators levied heavy fines, and in some cases lifetime trading suspensions, on the control group of brokers. The heaviest penalty was that paid by First Marathon, which never recovered its luster and ended up being saved by a Canadian Chartered Bank.

But there were others, lets just call them associates, who did very well and got to keep their profits and their livelihoods. These were the followers or listeners; those who were privy to the game going on at Cartaway, and who controlled small listed mining companies that could play along without breaking the eleventh commandment and getting caught. One or two of these companies staked claims near those owned by Cartaway and enjoyed huge increases in share values as the charade played out. It was like having someone out front to do the heavy lifting without all the risk and expense of actually exploring. Maybe these were the smart ones. They knew how the game was played, and lived to do it all again when the next great discovery comes along, as it surely will.

* * *

14

THE SKIN OF THE GODS:

Some 1500 years BC, Egyptian Royalty and other potentates were the exclusive owners of gold. They used the lustrous metal as a means of defining their power and importance, both in life and the afterlife. They believed that Gold, or Nubia, as it was called, was the skin of the Gods that would grant them immortality.

The Pharaohs would spend most of their short lives acquiring, by means of tribute or slavery, a hoard of highly refined gold that would later be used in their entombment. Many thousands of lives were expended in the production of 7 million ounces of gold from mines in Wadi in the Southern part of what is now Egypt. Very little of this gold has ever been found (that located in the Valley of the Kings being the exception) leaving scholars and the curious to wonder what happened to the rest. Since gold is nearly indestructible, and subject to theft, suspicion falls on the Romans, who conquered the Land of the Pharaohs and took tribute as payment for their legions.

The Romans had some very different ideas on the best uses of gold. They did not bury their dead in tombs and used gold instead as a pecuniary medium of exchange. Their idea of using coinage made from different metals would set them apart from the rest of the world and allow for a standard of living not seen again for a thousand years thereafter.

They created gold and silver coinage through a central mint in Rome. They established a fixed ratio first between gold and silver and then between bronze and copper coinage. This "specie," or payment in kind, allowed for greatly expanded trade and commerce as well as the movement of capital to and from Rome as the center of the Empire.

The whole system worked on trust. Trust that the "specie" created would in fact be exchangeable into a fixed amount of gold and silver. Unfortunately, the Romans would eventually pay a terrible price for the continued breach of this trust. The temptation to create ever-increasing amounts of "specie" without regard to the amount of gold available in Roman vaults was just too great. The legionnaires had to be paid, as did the growing numbers of functionaries required to keep the far-flung Empire in good order. In the absence of new conquests and new sources of gold and silver, regional governments resorted to the practice of debasing" or devaluing the currency. This practice would eventually bring down the Empire and re-introduce their citizens to serfdom.

It may well be that we, who do not heed the lessons of history, are doomed to relive it. For the failure to regulate the flow of "specie," or money, as we now call it, has led to an almost non-stop boom/bust cycle since the end of the Roman Empire. The one hundred year period of British Supremacy from 1815 to 1915 and the use of the Gold Standard are the exception.

Just like the Romans before them, British Bankers, led by N. M. Rothschild created and maintained a system of Bills of Exchange, which as the name implies, were exchangeable into gold, as was the hard currency minted in gold, silver, copper, and bronze. The Chartered Banks printed the heavily embossed notes that carried words to the effect of "a promise to pay on demand the sum of (pounds, shillings, and pence), all exchangeable into a fixed amount of gold." Following a few hiccups (the system was not perfect), the printing of notes was transferred to the control of the Bank of England, and the system spread to all points of the globe.

Again, it was trust that allowed the system to work so effectively. The neutrality and independence of the Bank of England were crucial to this trust, and the governments of the day were forced into fiscal discipline, a far cry from the reckless abandon of national treasuries today.

This wonderful system was brought low by the unmanageable debts run up by the Allies in the First World War. Chaos followed when governments broke the link between their currencies and gold and started printing "specie" to pay their debts. The euphoria of the 20's was followed by the Great Depression, which was followed once more by the inflation of War. And so the cycle has continued to this day.

A serious attempt to stop the cycle was made at the Breton Woods Economic Summit following the end of the Second World War. The American Delegation shot down a proposal made by Freidrich Hayek, a member of the Austrian School of Economists, to return to a modified form of the Gold Standard and the implied form of fiscal discipline. The Americans, who held all the cards, did not trust France and Britain to refrain from currency debasement as a means of paying their war debts, belief which would prove prophetic during the following three decades of the American Dollar hegemony.

Now it appears that the pot may well have been calling the kettle black, for it is the American dollar currently in danger of being devalued at the expense of the Europeans. The world is awash in dollars, in "specie" that has been printed to pay for Wars in the Middle East and the ever-increasing cost of bloated social programs.

At the time of Breton Woods, it took just US $35 to buy an ounce of gold. Now it takes $US 1300 to buy the same ounce. In 1941, the America Treasury owned nearly 650 million ounces of gold; now it owns only 147 million ounces. So who got the better deal, the seller or the buyer?

Goldfields are one of the oldest and most preeminent gold companies in the World. Based in South Africa, it was a founding member of the World Gold Council, and as such has done more than any other company to keep gold relevant in the age of "specie" and paper currency.

Once a year, Goldfields publishes The Gold Book, a massive tome that tries to make sense of gold as a commodity subject to supply and demand. The attempt works somewhat but falls short in explaining the rise and fall of gold values expressed in the major currencies of the world over time. The reason for this is that gold is not and never has been merely a commodity. It is rather an International Reserve Currency, albeit not one that is accepted many places as legal tender.

The great bulk of gold in the World is held in vaults, where it almost never sees the light of day. Annual production of new gold of a little less than 700 tons (22 million ounces) is small enough so as to make little difference to the demand that comes mainly from jewelry manufacturers, central banks, and the communications industry. Because of this paucity of supply, the "float" of physical metal is very small, a fact that can cause the London Market to be very volatile in everyday trading. The COMEX Futures Exchange in New York will normally follow London at the opening but frequently changes course during the trading session. This is because the time horizon for the trades is different. The Futures Market, stripped of all the hyperbole, is a bet on what the conversion rate between Gold and the US dollar will be at some point in the future. Very few of these contracts are settled by the exchange of metal. They are settled in dollars or another currency. So in simple terms, if a money manager believes that the purchasing power of the dollar will fall, he will go "long" on gold and "short" the Dollar. The only difference between this and many other forms of "hedging" as it is now called is that there are no "stops," or limits, on price movements in a trading session. This makes for a risky business, so the tool is used mainly by institutions for relatively short periods of time.

The continued likelihood of currency devaluation over a much longer period of time presents a far more difficult challenge for those who care about such things.

The first step in understanding must come from the realization that this is a "when" question (when will the next devaluation occur) rather than an "if" question (will a devaluation occur). Herein lies the reason for the dichotomy that shadows opinions about gold. About half of the world population, the "savers," believe in the "when" theory. The other half, the "spenders," believe in the "if" theory. Take for example the inhabitants of Formosa or Taiwan, who have a healthy distrust in their government's ability to look after them. They fear, rightly, that should the monster of Peking decide to take back its lost island, they would be left to fend for themselves. It is estimated that the Taiwanese own amounts of gold equivalent to four times the amount of "specie" in circulation. Normally such a skewed equation would render the local currency useless, since good money drives out bad money. The exception being that in this, case the "savers" are prepared to wait and see.

It is an open secret that the Monetary School of Economists (The Chicago School), who hold sway over the current polices of American and European Central Bankers, would like to get rid of gold altogether. They see it as the "dead" metal," a quaint relic from a bygone time. They believe that free markets and floating exchange rates will take care of the problems. They may well be right, except for the rather large problem of convincing the other half of the world of their ability to stop freely elected governments from continuing to debase their currencies. Unfortunately, recent history is not on their side.

In 1935, President Franklin Roosevelt, who apparently had a visceral dislike of Bankers, and his Democrat New Dealers passed into law the Gold Reserve Act. The Act fixed the value of gold at US $35 an ounce, outlawed the use of gold as legal tender and forbade American Citizens from owning large amounts of gold (bullion and coinage). Between 1935 and 1941, when America entered the War, the US Treasury printed $40 billion in "specie" (over 5 trillion in today's dollars) to acquire nearly 950 million ounces of gold stored at Fort Knox in Kentucky. The idea was to neutralize gold as a currency, discourage saving, and create inflation (as opposed to deflation).

Another experiment in gold neutralization happened in France. In the 1950's The French Government, saddled with huge war debts and a continuing War with Algerian Terrorists, was forced to keep devaluing the Franc. Then along came Charles De Gaulle who followed Roosevelt and purchased gold from French Citizens using 'New Devalued Francs' to create another great hoard of gold.

Both of these schemes may have worked for a short period of time, but they failed miserably to dim the allure of gold in the long term.

"The Nixon Shock," as it is was called, re-monetized gold by eliminating the US$ 35 fixed rate of exchange while at the same time as dumping the system of fixed exchange rates set up the Breton Woods Agreement. In any other terminology, Nixon's actions represented an acknowledgment of the fact that the dollar had already been devalued, for gold was unofficially valued in international markets at US $100 an ounce. It was about to get a lot worse.

The "Guns and Butter," policies of President Johnson's Great Society, launched during the War in Vietnam, had placed a huge strain on the finances of the nation, and the national debt grew at alarming rates. The Bond Market rebelled, causing interest rates to rise while gold values took off into the stratosphere. This was the first period of so called "stagflation," and it will not be the last.

The real shock in all of this was that America, like so many societies before it, did not possess the wealth to carry on wars while lavishing citizens with expensive social programs. The inability to raise taxes to finance these activities set in motion the death throes of the American dollar as the sole medium of exchange for international trade.

In the thirty intervening years, the situation has gotten a lot worse. The world is now awash in already devalued American dollars. It now takes 1300 new dollars to buy an ounce of gold as compared to 100 dollars in 1973. Many feel that the devaluation would have gone a lot further but for the comparison to the Euro that has been devaluing even faster, and for the innate distrust of the Chinese Proletariat to provide an alternative.

So it appears as though the "when" believers are already well ahead of the "if" believers. But the battle is far from over. Because of the huge overhang of the American National Debt (now at $US 14 trillion and counting), chances are good that history will once again repeat and this debt will be serviced by another round of New Dollars.

The next batch of New Dollars will most likely come from a new world order of currency alignment, one that may well give credence to Frederich Hayek's concept of linking the various printed "specie" to a basket of commodities and currencies. Such a basket will include gold and silver but not to the extent of a return to the Gold Standard, and with a much lower weighting for gold than the "when" believers would want.

This rather gloomy forecast does not bode well for gold-mining companies, because as with The Gold Reserve Act, the mere act of marginalizing gold is likely to depress the demand for the metal in the short term. This may not be such a bad thing because the method of evaluating these companies has always been highly suspect. They are seen by believers to be a store of value, equivalent to the ounces of gold in the ground discounted over the expected rate of production. The historical fallacy is that the miners can produce the gold faster than the rising costs of doing so, and that they can avoid stupid mistakes in replacing their reserves.

It remains far better to buy the metal than to buy the producer. The trick is to find a cheap method of owning and storing a currency that is extremely prone to theft and swindle.

It appears as though the World Gold Council, after years of struggle, may have found a method for the average "when" believer to place part of their savings in physical gold. They achieved this feat by instituting a direct look-alike to the Bills of Exchange issued and maintained by British Chartered Banks in the early years of the 19th Century. By guaranteeing the supply of gold, they made possible the ETF (Exchange Traded Fund, ticker Symbol g.o.l.d.) that is directly exchangeable into a fixed amount of gold.

Many such funds now exist all over the world in different currencies. Effective arbitrage between the various Exchanges now keeps the "bid" and "ask' prices very close the equivalent London and New York values.

Because these funds have become so popular, it is almost inconceivable that they will be ignored in the coming currency re-alignment. Perhaps they will have to be redeemed, but history tells us that gold itself is unlikely to go away for very long.

* * *

EPILOGUE:

THE EXCITING DAYS OF THE LAST GOLD RUSH are now a part of history. There is a saying among gold miners that the "easy gold" has all been found, a belief that leads to another saying, that most new gold mines are found on top of or near old gold mines. Easy or not, it is now much harder to make a gold mine than it ever was. Stricter environmental regulations and higher wage costs have tempered the enthusiasm of all but the most intrepid of miners.

How long this intransigence will last remains to be seen. My bet would be only until the next big discovery and a renewal of gold fever.

The Wharf Mine that is at the center of my experience in the gold business is now a part of Goldcorp, the most profitable gold-mining company in the world. In the twenty-seven intervening years, the mine has produced over two million ounces of gold at enormous profit to its owners, and promises to yield a lot more in the future. It shames me to relate that if, my miner friends, and I had bought this great deposit, I would not have written this tale.

Homestake Mining was taken over by Barrick Gold, the largest gold-mining company in the world. The famous Homestake mine in South Dakota was closed and now acts as a research facility trying to isolate Dark Matter in the Universe.

Pegasus Gold declared bankruptcy and its gold mines are now owned by its bondholders.

Samuel Montagu is now owned by HSBC, the giant Hong Kong Bank, now based in London.

"Sell-the-Pig Jim" was fined an enormous sum by regulators for allowing a bond manipulation scheme and was forced to end his imaginative trading career.

"The Shark" took his fortune and disappeared back into the shadows from whence he came.

The mines at Hemlo produced over twenty-two million ounces of gold, making this discovery one of the most prolific in Canadian history.

Murray Pezim, the stock promoter who started the great Hemlo gold rush, has gone on to his reward and is now enshrined in the Canadian Mining Hall of Fame.

The dealmaker who made it all happen, and who was kind enough to tell me the story, now lives in California.

The Hemlo legal decision that survived appeals to the Supreme Court of Canada is now enshrined in Canadian Common Law.

It is the surviving legacy of "The Monk", that he was able to raise the vast sum of money required to rectify his folly through the sale of new shares, thereby replacing almost the entire equity value of his company. The accountants and auditors walked free, saved by arcane disclosures as notes to financial statements understood by almost no one.

The Busang story remains unresolved as the biggest mining fraud ever perpetuated. Many of the participants are now deceased, and the case is officially closed.

John, the Dutch geologist, a major participant, was found not guilty of insider trading and now owns a general store in Borneo. No one else has ever been charged with any crime.

NOTES:

www.ingramcontent.com/pod-product-compliance
Lightning Source LLC
Chambersburg PA
CBHW080643180526
45168CB00008B/3281